SPRINTS AND DISTANCES

SPRINTS AND

SPORTS IN POETRY AND

Compiled by Lillian Morrison

Illustrated by Clare and John Ross

DISTANCES

THE POETRY IN SPORT

Thomas Y. Crowell Company   New York

BOOKS BY THE AUTHOR

Yours Till Niagara Falls
Black Within and Red Without
A Diller, A Dollar: Rhymes and Sayings
for the Ten O'Clock Scholar
Touch Blue
Remember Me When This You See
Sprints and Distances

To the two sportsmen in my life
Milt *and* Al
and to the rest of my sports-loving family
Mary
Muriel, Rob, *and* Danny

FOREWORD

THERE IS an affinity between sports and poetry. Each is a form of play; each is a form of ritual. Each has the power to take us out of ourselves and at times to lift us above ourselves. They go together naturally wherever there is zest for life. The ancient Greeks, with their great athletic festivals presided over by the Muses, exalted both. And Robert Frost once said, "I go so far as to connect all of the sports with poetry."

For most sports lovers the action, the game, the passion, the movement are poetry enough. This collection celebrates that "poetry." But I have also selected these poems hoping that the sports-loving reader might discover, perhaps for the first time, the poetry and power of words as well. Many of the poems here will express his sensations and experiences, some will make him laugh, and many, as in the last three sections of the book, will explore other aspects of life, death, and feeling in a way especially meaningful for him—through the sport metaphor. Such a reader is particularly fitted to read poetry as it should be read—with the muscles (actually sensing the movement and rhythm and moving inwardly with it) as well as with the eye, ear, and mind.

As for the poetry lover who has little taste for sports, I hope that the poets here may make him see what he never saw in sports before: rhythm, grace, form, precision—in short, "poetry in motion" and the skill and dedication required to achieve it. He may discover that the reflections of the quiet sportsman—the hiker, the fisherman, the lonely swimmer—are much like his own, and he may recognize too in the emotions of athlete and spectator those high moments which have always moved poets to write.

Of course, those who enjoy both sports and poetry can find a unique satisfaction in reading a good poem about a favorite sport. And for those who like neither (and will probably never be reading these pages) there is always the hope that they take pleasure in nature, music, art, or are fortunate in love. For the man with no poetry in his life is a dead man.

Lillian Morrison

PREFATORY NOTE

THE POEMS included here range from memorable newspaper verse to pieces by Pindar, Virgil, Wordsworth, and Yeats. They vary in form from simple quatrains to intricate modern verse. No attempt was made to include every sport though many are represented, from baseball to falconry. Nor are all the poems in praise of sport. Some are critical, some satiric. The only measures for selection were the quality and appeal of the poems themselves. Although some of the football poems refer to the British form of the game (similar to our soccer) emphasis in the collection is on sports known and practiced in the United States.

I am grateful to many people for help in the making of this book—to my publishers, for patience, as well as for useful ideas; to Miss Amelia Munson, who read a large part of the manuscript, for appreciative encouragement and good suggestions; and to Miss Louise Mead, member of the 1959 Pan-American track team, for refreshing criticism of the poems on running. I am also indebted to many people, the following in particular, for various kindnesses, from suggesting sources of poems to lending me books: Miss Babette Deutsch, Mr. Gerald McDonald, Mrs. Marian C. O'Donnell, Mrs. Ruth Rausen, Miss Rose Rosberg, Mr. Ben Shahn, and Mr. William Sloan.

CONTENTS

The Games

"What work's, my countrymen, in hand?
        Where go you
With bats and clubs?"

WILLIAM SHAKESPEARE

The Base Stealer

Poised between going on and back, pulled
Both ways taut like a tightrope-walker,
Fingertips pointing the opposites,
Now bouncing tiptoe like a dropped ball
Or a kid skipping rope, come on, come on,
Running a scattering of steps sidewise,
How he teeters, skitters, tingles, teases,
Taunts them, hovers like an ecstatic bird,
He's only flirting, crowd him, crowd him,
Delicate, delicate, delicate, delicate—now!

ROBERT FRANCIS

Baseball Note

In winter, when it's cold out,
Appears the baseball holdout;
In spring, when it is warm out,
He gets his uniform out.

FRANKLIN P. ADAMS

2

Hits and Runs

I remember the Chillicothe ball players grappling the Rock
    Island ball players in a sixteen-inning game ended by
    darkness.

And the shoulders of the Chillicothe players were a red smoke
    against the sundown and the shoulders of the Rock
    Island players were a yellow smoke against the sun-
    down.

And the umpire's voice was hoarse calling balls and strikes and
    outs, and the umpire's throat fought in the dust for a
    song.

CARL SANDBURG

Pitcher

His art is eccentricity, his aim
How not to hit the mark he seems to aim at,

His passion how to avoid the obvious,
His technique how to vary the avoidance.

The others throw to be comprehended. He
Throws to be a moment misunderstood.

Yet not too much. Not errant, arrant, wild,
But every seeming aberration willed.

Not to, yet still, still to communicate
Making the batter understand too late.

ROBERT FRANCIS

The Umpire

The umpire is a lonely man
Whose calls are known to every fan
Yet none will call him Dick or Dan
    In all the season's games.
They'll never call him Al or Ed
Or Bill or Phil or Frank or Fred
Or Jim or Tim or Tom or Ted—
    They'll simply call him names.

MILTON BRACKER

The Umpire

Everyone knows he's blind as a bat.
Besides, it's tricky to decide,
As ball meets mitt with a loud splat,
Whether it curved an inch outside
Or just an inch the other way
For a called strike. But anyway,
Nobody thinks that just because
Instead he calls that close one Ball,
That that was what it really *was*.
(The pitcher doesn't agree at all.)

His eyes are weak, his vision's blurred,
He can't tell a strike from a barn door—
And yet we have to take his word.
The pitch that was something else before
(And *there's* the mystery no one knows)
Has gotten to be a ball by now,
Or got to be called ball, anyhow.
All this explains why, I suppose,
People like to watch baseball games,
Where Things are not confused with Names.

WALKER GIBSON

Decline and Fall of a Roman Umpire

I sing of Tony Caesar, a big league arbiter of unimpeachable
    repute
Except for one impeacher, who was a beaut.
Tony dreaded each new season because whenever behind third
    base at the Stadium he took his stand
This impeacher was on hand.
He had a cowbell and a bull voice,
And his vocabulary, though limited, was far from choice.
It beat on Tony's ears like a savage drum:
Caesar, ya big bum ya, you're nothing but a big bum!
Sometimes he would crummily roar, Caesar, you ain't no
    umpire,
You're a bumpire!
Sometimes he would roar something even crummier,
But mostly he just roared, Oh ya big bum, ya big bum ya!

Tony was really as saintly a man as Dr. Jekyll,
But the more his heckler continued to heckle,
Why the more he began to feel like Mr. Hyde,
Until one day he decided to have his heckler private-eyed,
And when the private eye turned in his report, well the next
    time Tony was called a bum,
He walked over to his tormentor and mildly said, Come, come!
I am reliably informed that you have one wife in Brooklyn, one
    in the Bronx, and a lady friend in Queens;
Your first conviction was for robbing a blind vendor of news-
    papers and magazines;
Your other offenses range from drunk and disorderly to pocket-
    picking, automobile theft and arson,

As well as making off with the poor box after brutally assaulting
the parson.
I suggest, sir, that you take heed;
Who is calling whom a bum, yes, whom indeed?
To which the snarled reply was, Aah, get your eye out of
my thumb;
I'm calling *you* a bum, ya big bum!
Tony gave up and abandoned the big leagues for the Little
League and changed his name to Tittelbaum,
And he is happy now because the spectators only call him a
little bum.

OGDEN NASH

Polo Grounds

Time is of the essence. This is a highly skilled
And beautiful mystery. Three or four seconds only
From the time that Riggs connects till he reaches first,
And in those seconds Jurges goes to his right,
Comes up with the ball, tosses to Witek at second
For the force on Reese, Witek to Mize at first,
In time for the out—a double play.

(Red Barber crescendo. Crowd noises, obbligato;
Scattered staccatos from the peanut boys,
Loud in the lull, as the teams are changing sides) . . .

Hubbell takes the sign, nods, pumps, delivers—
A foul into the stands. Dunn takes a new ball out,
Hands it to Danning, who throws it down to Werber;
Werber takes off his glove, rubs the ball briefly,
Tosses it over to Hub, who goes to the rosin bag,
Takes the sign from Danning, pumps, delivers—
Low, outside, ball three. Danning goes to the mound,
Says something to Hub. Dunn brushes off the plate,
Adams starts throwing in the Giant bull pen,
Hub takes the sign from Danning, pumps, delivers,
Camilli gets hold of it, a *long* fly to the outfield,
Ott goes back, back, back, against the wall, gets under it,
Pounds his glove, and takes it for the out.
That's all for the Dodgers. . . .

Time is of the essence. The rhythms break,
More varied and subtle than any kind of dance;

Movement speeds up or lags. The ball goes out
In sharp and angular drives, or long, slow arcs,
Comes in again controlled and under aim;
The players wheel or spurt, race, stoop, slide, halt,
Shift imperceptibly to new positions,
Watching the signs, according to the batter,
The score, the inning. Time is of the essence.

Time is of the essence. Remember Terry?
Remember Stonewall Jackson, Lindstrom, Frisch,
When they were good? Remember Long George Kelly?
Remember John McGraw and Benny Kauff?
Remember Bridwell, Tenney, Merkle, Youngs,
Chief Myers, Big Jeff Tesreau, Shufflin' Phil?
Remember Matthewson, and Ames, and Donlin,
Buck Ewing, Rusie, Smiling Mickey Welch?
Remember a left-handed catcher named Jack Humphries,
Who sometimes played the outfield, in '83?

Time is of the essence. The shadow moves
From the plate to the box, from the box to second base,
From second to the outfield, to the bleachers.

Time is of the essence. The crowd and players
Are the same age always, but the man in the crowd
Is older every season. Come on, play ball!

ROLFE HUMPHRIES

Casey at the Bat

The outlook wasn't brilliant for the Mudville nine that day;
The score stood four to two with but one inning more to play.
And then, when Cooney died at first, and Barrows d   ,
A sickly silence fell upon the patrons of the game.

A straggling few got up to go in deep despair. The rest
Clung to that hope which springs eternal in the human b
They thought, If only Casey could but get a whack at that
We'd put up even money now, with Casey at the bat.

But Flynn preceded Casey, as did also Jimmy Blake,
And the former was a lulu and the latter was a cake;
So upon that stricken multitude grim melancholy sat,
For there seemed but little chance of Casey's getting to the bat.

But Flynn let drive a single, to the wonderment of all,
And Blake, the much despisèd, tore the cover off the ball;
And when the dust had lifted, and men saw what had occurred,
There was Jimmy safe at second, and Flynn a-hugging third.

Then from five thousand throats and more there rose a lusty
        yell;
It rumbled through the valley, it rattled in the dell;
It knocked upon the mountain and recoiled upon the flat,
For Casey, mighty Casey, was advancing to the bat.

There was ease in Casey's manner as he stepped into his place;
There was pride in Casey's bearing and a smile on Casey's face.
And when, responding to the cheers, he lightly doffed his hat,
No stranger in the crowd could doubt 'twas Casey at the bat.

Ten thousand eyes were on him as he rubbed his hands with
 dirt,
Five thousand tongues applauded when he wiped them on his
 shirt;
Then while the writhing pitcher ground the ball into his hip,
Defiance gleamed from Casey's eye, a sneer curled Casey's lip.

And now the leather-covered sphere came hurtling through the
 air,
And Casey stood a-watching it in haughty grandeur there.
Close by the sturdy batsman the ball unheeded sped;
"That ain't my style," said Casey. "Strike one," the umpire said.

From the benches, black with people, there went up a muffled
 roar,
Like the beating of the storm waves on a stern and distant
 shore.
"Kill him! Kill the umpire!" shouted someone on the stand;
And it's likely they'd have killed him had not Casey raised his
 hand.

With a smile of Christian charity great Casey's visage shone;
He stilled the rising tumult, he bade the game go on;
He signaled to the pitcher, and once more the spheroid flew;
But Casey still ignored it, and the umpire said, "Strike two."

"Fraud!" cried the maddened thousands, and echo answered
 "Fraud!"
But one scornful look from Casey and the audience was awed;
They saw his face grow stern and cold, they saw his muscles
 strain,
And they knew that Casey wouldn't let that ball go by again.

The sneer is gone from Casey's lip, his teeth are clenched in
      hate,
He pounds with cruel violence his bat upon the plate;
And now the pitcher holds the ball, and now he lets it go,
And now the air is shattered by the force of Casey's blow.

Oh, somewhere in this favored land the sun is shining bright,
The band is playing somewhere, and somewhere hearts are
      light;
And somewhere men are laughing, and somewhere children
      shout,
But there is no joy in Mudville—mighty Casey has struck out.

ERNEST LAWRENCE THAYER

Baseball's Sad Lexicon

These are the saddest of possible words:
    "Tinker to Evers to Chance."
Trio of bear cubs, and fleeter than birds,
    Tinker and Evers and Chance.
Ruthlessly pricking our gonfalon bubble,
Making a Giant hit into a double—
Words that are heavy with nothing but trouble:
    "Tinker to Evers to Chance."

FRANKLIN P. ADAMS

Cobb Would Have Caught It

In sunburnt parks where Sundays lie,
Or the wide wastes beyond the cities,
Teams in grey deploy through sunlight.

Talk it up, boys, a little practice.

Coming in stubby and fast, the baseman
Gathers a grounder in fat green grass,
Picks it stinging and clipped as wit
Into the leather: a swinging step
Wings it deadeye down to first.
Smack. Oh, attaboy, attyoldboy.

Catcher reverses his cap, pulls down
Sweaty casque, and squats in the dust:
Pitcher rubs new ball on his pants,
Chewing, puts a jet behind him;
Nods past batter, taking his time.
Batter settles, tugs at his cap:
A spinning ball: step and swing to it,
Caught like a cheek before it ducks
By shivery hickory: socko, baby:
Cleats dig into the dust. Outfielder,
On his way, looking over shoulder,
Makes it a triple. A long peg home.

Innings and afternoons. Fly lost in sunset.
Throwing arm gone bad. There's your old ball game.
Cool reek of the field. Reek of companions.

ROBERT FITZGERALD

15

The Double-Play

In his sea lit
distance, the pitcher winding
like a clock about to chime comes down with

the ball, hit
sharply, under the artificial
banks of arc-lights, bounds like a vanishing string

over the green
to the shortstop magically
scoops to his right whirling above his invisible

shadows
in the dust redirects
its flight to the running poised second baseman

pirouettes
leaping, above the slide, to throw
from mid-air, across the colored tightened interval,

to the leaning-
out first baseman ends the dance
drawing it disappearing into his long brown glove

stretches. What
is too swift for deception
is final, lost, among the loosened figures

jogging off the field
(the pitcher walks), casual
in the space where the poem has happened.

ROBERT WALLACE

Dream of a Baseball Star

I dreamed Ted Williams
leaning at night
against the Eiffel Tower, weeping.

He was in uniform
and his bat lay at his feet
—knotted and twiggy.

'Randall Jarrell says you're a poet!' I cried.
'So do I! I say you're a poet!'

He picked up his bat with blown hands;
stood there astraddle as he would in the batter's box,
and laughed! flinging his schoolboy wrath
toward some invisible pitcher's mound
—waiting the pitch all the way from heaven.

It came; hundreds came! all afire!
He swung and swung and swung and connected not one
sinker curve hook or right-down-the-middle.
A hundred strikes!
The umpire dressed in strange attire
thundered his judgment: YOU'RE OUT!
And the phantom crowd's horrific boo
dispersed the gargoyles from Notre Dame.

And I screamed in my dream:
God! throw thy merciful pitch!
Herald the crack of bats!
Hooray the sharp liner to left!
Yea the double, the triple!
Hosannah the home run!

GREGORY CORSO

To Satch (or American Gothic)

Sometimes I feel like I will *never* stop
Just go on forever
Till one fine mornin
I'm gonna reach up and grab me a handfulla stars
Swing out my long lean leg
And whip three hot strikes burnin down the heavens
And look over at God and say
How about that!

SAMUEL ALLEN

18

To Lou Gehrig

We've been to the wars together;
We took our foes as they came;
And always you were the leader,
And ever you played the game.

Idol of cheering millions,
  Records are yours by sheaves;
Iron of frame they hailed you,
  Decked you with laurel leaves.
But higher than that we hold you,
  We who have known you best,
Knowing the way you came through
  Every human test.

Let this be a silent token
Of lasting friendship's gleam
And all that we've left unspoken—
Your pals of the Yankee team.

JOHN KIERAN

This was written at the request of Gehrig's teammates
and inscribed on a trophy which they gave him on
    "Gehrig Day" about a year before he died.—L.M.

Where, O Where?

Where are the heroes of yesteryear?
Has ever their like been seen?
    Terry and Gehrig and Melvin Ott
    Lining another one out of the lot—
And Harry (The Cat) Brecheen.

Where are the stars of my misspent youth—
Like Meusel and Frisch, I mean?
    Tony Lazzeri (before Di Mag)
    Leading the Yanks to a runaway flag—
And Harry (The Cat) Brecheen.

Where are the players I loved so well—
Art Nehf, and the Brothers Dean?
    Who in the multitude does not miss
    Walter and Alex and Tyrus and Tris—
And Harry (The Cat) Brecheen?

MILTON BRACKER

Line-Up for Yesterday

AN ABC OF BASEBALL IMMORTALS

A is for Alex,
The great Alexander;
More goose eggs he pitched
Than a popular gander.

B is for Bresnahan
Back of the plate;
The Cubs were his love,
And McGraw was his hate.

C is for Cobb,
Who grew spikes and not corn,
And made all the basemen
Wish they weren't born.

D is for Dean,
The grammatical Diz,
When they asked, Who's the tops?
Said correctly, I is.

E is for Evers,
His jaw in advance;
Never afraid
To Tinker with Chance.

F is for Fordham
And Frankie and Frisch;
I wish he were back
With the Giants, I wish.

G is for Gehrig,
The pride of the Stadium;
His record pure gold,
His courage, pure radium.

H is for Hornsby;
When pitching to Rog,
The pitcher would pitch,
Then the pitcher would dodge.

I is for Me,
Not a hard-sitting man,
But an outstanding all-time
Incurable fan.

J is for Johnson.
The Big Train in his prime
Was so fast he could throw
Three strikes at a time.

K is for Keeler,
As fresh as green paint,
The fustest and mostest
To hit where they ain't.

L is Lajoie,
Whom Clevelanders love,

Napoleon himself,
With glue in his glove.

M is for Matty,
Who carried a charm
In the form of an extra
Brain in his arm.

N is for Newsom,
Bobo's favorite kin.
If you ask how he's here,
He talked himself in.

O is for Ott
Of the restless right foot.
When he leaned on the pellet,
The pellet stayed put.

P is for Plank,
The arm of the A's;
When he tangled with Matty
Games lasted for days.

Q is Don Quixote
Cornelius Mack;
Neither Yankees nor Years
Can halt his attack.

R is for Ruth.
To tell you the truth,
There's no more to be said,
Just R is for Ruth.

S is for Speaker,
Swift center-field tender;
When the ball saw him coming,
It yelled "I surrender."

T is for Terry,
The Giant from Memphis,
Whose 400 average
You can't overemphis.

U would be 'Ubbell
If Carl were a cockney;
We say Hubbell and baseball
Like football and Rockne.

V is for Vance,
The Dodgers' own Dazzy;
None of his rivals
Could throw as fast as he.

W, Wagner,
The bowlegged beauty;
Short was closed to all traffic
With Honus on duty.

X is the first
Of two x's in Foxx,
Who was right behind Ruth
With his powerful soxx.

Y is for Young
The magnificent Cy;

People batted against him,
But I never knew why.

Z is for Zenith,
The summit of fame.
These men are up there,
These men are the game.

OGDEN NASH

Second Half

Shadows are long on Soldiers Field,
Where some of us sit half congealed.
Nature, it seems, the greatest Healer,
Is even greater as Congealer.

DAVID MC CORD

Football

The Game was ended, and the noise
at last had died away, and now they
gathered up the boys where they in
pieces lay. And one was hammered in the
ground by many a jolt and jar; some frag-
ments never have been found, they flew
away so far. They found a stack of tawny
hair, some fourteen cubits high; it was the
half-back, lying there, where he had
crawled to die. They placed the pieces on
a door, and from the crimson field, that
hero then they gently bore, like soldier on
his shield. The surgeon toiled the livelong
night above the gory wreck; he got the
ribs adjusted right, the wishbone and the
neck. He soldered on the ears and toes,
and got the spine in place, and fixed a gutta-
percha nose upon the mangled face. And
then he washed his hands and said: "I'm
glad that task is done!" The half-back
raised his fractured head, and cried: "I
call this fun!"

WALT MASON

The Passer

Dropping back with the ball ripe in my palm,
grained and firm as the flesh of a living charm,
I taper and coil myself down, raise arm to fake,
running a little, seeing my targets emerge
like quail above a wheat field's golden lake.

In boyhood I saw my mother knit my warmth
with needles that were straight. I learned to feel
the passage of the bullet through the bore,
its vein of flight between my heart and deer
whose terror took the pulse of my hot will.

I learned how wild geese slice arcs from hanging pear
of autumn noon; how the thought of love cleaves home,
and fists, with fury's ray, can lay a weakness bare,
and instinct's eye can mine fish under foam.

So as I run and weigh, measure and test,
the light kindles on helmets, the angry leap;
but secretly, coolly, as though stretching a hand to his chest,
I lay the ball in the arms of my planing end,
as true as metal, as deftly as surgeon's wrist.

GEORGE ABBE

Football Song

Then strip, lads, and to it, though sharp be the weather,
  And if, by mischance, you should happen to fall,
There are worse things in life than a tumble on heather,
  And life is itself but a game at football.

And when it is over, we'll drink a blithe measure
  To each Laird and each Lady that witnessed our fun,
And to every blithe heart that took part in our pleasure,
  To the lads that have lost and the lads that have won.

CHORUS

Then up with the Banner, let forest winds fan her,
  She has blazed over Ettrick eight ages and more;
In sport we'll attend her, in battle defend her,
  With heart and with hand, like our fathers before.

SIR WALTER SCOTT

Heaps on Heaps

And now both Bands in close embraces met,
Now foot to foot, and breast to breast was set.
Now all impatient grapple round the Ball,
And Heaps on Heaps in wild Disorder fall.

MATTHEW CONCANEN
from A Match at Football
(1721)

The Dangers of Foot-ball

Where Covent-Garden's famous temple stands,
That boasts the work of Jones' immortal hands,
Columns with plain magnificence appear,
And graceful porches lead along the square:
Here oft' my course I bend, when lo! from far
I spy the furies of the foot-ball war:
The 'prentice quits his shop, to join the crew,
Increasing crowds the flying game pursue.
Thus, as you roll the ball o'er snowy ground,
The gath'ring globe augments with every round.
But whither shall I run? The throng draws nigh,
The ball now skims the street, now soars on high;
The dext'rous glazier strong returns the bound,
And gingling sashes on the pent-house sound.

JOHN GAY
from Trivia; or, The Art of
Walking the Streets of London
(1716)

Settling Some Old Football Scores

This is the football hero's moment of fame.
   Glory is his, though erstwhile he may have shunned it.
In hall and street he hears the crying of his name
   By youth and maiden, alumnus and radio pundit.

Fierce on the newspaper pages his features show
   He smites his foe in the innumerable cinema
And in a myriad maidens' dreams. But oh,
   In literature his fame has reached its minima!

See, in the Broadway drama, what he has become, he
   Who was triply-threatening All-American!
He is a lubberly fellow, a downright dummy!
   And serious fiction is what he is frankly barbaric in.

We read of him telling victories won of yore,
   We see him vainly pursue fame's fleeting bubble;
The maid he adores is certain to leave him for
   A small dark wiry person, the author's double!

O football hero! Now while a million throats
   Acclaim thy glorious deeds, just set this much down:
A small dark wiry person is taking notes.
   Literature will make the ultimate touchdown.

MORRIS BISHOP

The Man from Inversnaid

IMITATED FROM WORDSWORTH

He brought a team from Inversnaid
  To play our Third Fifteen,
A man whom none of us had played
  And very few had seen.

He weighed not less than eighteen stone,
  And to a practiced eye
He seemed as little fit to run
  As he was fit to fly.

He looked so clumsy and so slow,
  And made so little fuss;
But he got in behind—and oh,
  The difference to us!

ROBERT FULLER MURRAY

31

A Ballade of Lawn Tennis

Some gain a universal fame
   By dint of pugilistic might;
To some all sports seem very tame
   Except a fierce and fistic fight;
   Some love the tourney, too, in spite
Of ancient armour, helm, and crest,
   Where knights are smitten and do smite—
I like the Game of Tennis best.

Some love to take a gun and aim
   At pretty birdlings in their flight;
Some also think it is no shame
   To make poor trout and pickerel bite;
   Some chase the deer from morn till night—
I like not such a bloody quest,
   My sport is harmless, pleasant, light—
I like the Game of Tennis best.

Some for the ancient, royal game
   Of golf. Arrayed in colours bright
They'll play until they're sore and lame—
   A frenzy without justice, quite.
   Baseball and football may have right,
Polo and cricket and the rest
   Of sports too many to recite—
I like the Game of Tennis best.

Queen of the Court, my skill is slight
    In rhyming, but, perhaps you've guessed
Why this ballade I thus indite—
    I like the Game of Tennis best.

FRANKLIN P. ADAMS

From Adulescentia

Miraculously, through prayer to Saint Anthony,
The lost tennis ball was found in the alders:
That dun, worn, airy to-be-bounced
Treasurable and humble dweller in closets.

ROBERT FITZGERALD

The Olympic Girl

The sort of girl I like to see
Smiles down from her great height at me.
She stands in strong, athletic pose
And wrinkles her *retroussé* nose.
Is it distaste that makes her frown,
So furious and freckled, down
On an unhealthy worm like me?
Or am I what she likes to see?
I do not know, though much I care.
εἴθε γενοίμην . . . would I were
(Forgive me, shade of Rupert Brooke)
An object fit to claim her look.
Oh! would I were her racket press'd
With hard excitement to her breast
And swished into the sunlit air
Arm-high above her tousled hair,
And banged against the bounding ball
"Oh! Plung!" my tauten'd strings would call,
"Oh, Plung! my darling, break my strings
For you I will do brilliant things."
And when the match is over, I
Would flop beside you, hear you sigh;
And then, with what supreme caress,
You'ld tuck me up into my press.
Fair tigress of the tennis courts,
So short in sleeve and strong in shorts,
Little, alas, to you I mean,
For I am bald and old and green.

JOHN BETJEMAN

A Snapshot for Miss Bricka Who Lost in the Semi-Final Round of the Pennsylvania Lawn Tennis Tournament at Haverford, July, 1960

Applause flutters onto the open air
like starlings bursting from a frightened elm,
and swings away across the lawns
in the sun's green continuous calm

of far July. Coming off the court,
you drop your racket by the judge's tower
and towel your face, alone, looking off,
while someone whispers to the giggling winner,

and the crowd rustles, awning'd in tiers
or under umbrellas at court-end tables,
glittering like a carnival
against the mute distance of maples

along their strumming street beyond
the walls of afternoon. Bluely, loss
hurts in your eyes—not loss merely,
but seeing how everything is less

that seemed so much, how life moves on
past either defeat or victory,
how, too old to cry, you shall find steps
to turn away. Now others volley

behind you in the steady glare;
the crowd waits in its lazy revel,

holding whiskey sours, talking, pointing,
whose lives (like yours) will not unravel

to a backhand, a poem, or a sunrise,
though they may wish for it. The sun
brandishes softly his swords of light
on faces, grass, and sky. You'll win

hereafter, other days, when time
is kinder than this worn July
that keeps you like a snapshot: losing,
your eyes, once, made you beautiful.

ROBERT WALLACE

Tennis in San Juan

Thin under the arc lights,
Pin legs in their chalk whites;
The bug of the slammed ball
Trying in vain to get out;
All done in a slow dance
To night tune of the tree frog,
An inch long, glass, *co-kí*,
co-kí he says, *co-kí*,
Never seen but heard now,

Heard then, heard and heard
After the sundown, all night.

When the ball goes *co-kí*,
The tree frog says: *co-kí*,
Much Sabby, good stroke,
Señor Spalding, strong gut,
Like a firework, long lob,
With muscle guitar, good slam,
On C sharp, a good ping,
High the way the girls sing
Dancing the momba in Bay View
With tales told to just you.

Down at the dock they work ship,
Off the shore they see shark,
Under the reef they pull shell,
Into the boat they haul eel;
Up at the tennis, same way,
Professors work with white ball
Very hard, bang, bang
Lecturing night with hard work,
Possessing dark with hard play,
Under the arcs, with *co-kí*
Who also works with much breath.
So many ways they say love
So many ways they say death,
Up in the tennis tree, *co-kí*.

REUEL DENNEY

At the Tennis Clinic

There was a young man from Port Jervis
Who developed a marvelous service
But was sorry he learned it
For if someone returned it
It made him impossibly nervous.

I. L. MARTIN

Dark Eyes at Forest Hills

He gazed at her with his whole soul;
His look contained his all,
For she was the nearest linesman
And he didn't like the call.

I. L. MARTIN

Seaside Golf

How straight it flew, how long it flew,
It cleared the rutty track
And soaring, disappeared from view
Beyond the bunker's back—
A glorious, sailing, bounding drive
That made me glad I was alive.

And down the fairway, far along
It glowed a lovely white;
I played an iron sure and strong
And clipp'd it out of sight,
And spite of grassy banks between
I knew I'd find it on the green.

And so I did. It lay content
Two paces from the pin;
A steady putt and then it went
Oh, most securely in.
The very turf rejoiced to see
That quite unprecedented three.

Ah! seaweed smells from sandy caves
And thyme and mist in whiffs,
In-coming tide, Atlantic waves
Slapping the sunny cliffs,
Lark song and sea sounds in the air
And splendor, splendor everywhere.

JOHN BETJEMAN

Mullion

My ball is in a bunch of fern,
    A jolly place to be;
An angry man is close astern—
    He waves his club at me.
Well, let him wave—the sky is blue;
Go on, old ball, we are but two—
    We may be down in three,
Or nine—or ten—or twenty-five—
It matters not; to be alive
    Is good enough for me.

How like the happy sheep we pass
    At random through the green,
For ever in the longest grass,
    But never in between!
There is a madness in the air;
There is a damsel over there,
    Her ball is in the brook.
Ah! what a shot—a dream, a dream!
You think it finished in the stream?
    Well, well, we'll go and look.

Who is this hot and hasty man
    That shouteth 'Fore!' and 'Fore!'?
We move as quickly as we can—
    Can any one do more?
Cheer up, sweet sir, enjoy the view;
I'd take a seat if I were you,
    And light your pipe again:

In quiet thought possess your soul,
For John is down a rabbit hole,
    And I am down a drain.

The ocean is a lovely sight,
    A brig is in the bay.
Was that a slice? You may be right—
    But goodness, what a day!
Young men and maidens dot the down,
And they are beautiful and brown,
    And just as mad as me.
Sing, men and maids, for I have done
The Tenth—the Tenth!—in twenty-one,
    And John was twenty-three.

Now I will take my newest ball,
    And build a mighty tee,
And waggle once, or not at all,
    And bang it out to sea,
And hire a boat and bring it back,
And give it one terrific whack,
    And hole it out in three,
Or nine—or ten—or twenty-five—
It matters not; to be alive
At Mullion in the summer time,
At Mullion in the silly time,
    Is good enough for me.

A. P. HERBERT

Golfers

Like Sieur Montaigne's distinction
between virtue and innocence
what gets you is their unbewilderment

They come into the picture suddenly
like unfinished houses, gapes and planed wood,
dominating a landscape

And you see at a glance
among sportsmen they are the metaphysicians,
intent, untalkative, pursuing Unity
(What finally gets you is their chastity)

And that no theory of pessimism is complete
which altogether ignores them

IRVING LAYTON

42

A *Public Nuisance*

You know the fellow,
I have no doubt,
Who stands and waggles
His club about.

Empires crumble
And crowns decay;
Kings and Communists
Pass away.

Dictators rise
And dictators fall—
But *still* he stands
Addressing his ball.

REGINALD ARKELL

Afforestation

A waggish friend of the writer's suggested the other day how interesting it would be if, on any ordinary golf links, a tree could be made to spring up by magic on the spot where somebody had cheated.

Colonel B.
Drove from the tee;
Fell in a bunker—play'd two and play'd three;
Four, and then out.
Then, with a clout,
(Due to impatience and chagrin, no doubt)
Sent the ball speeding far over the green,
Into a drain.—
At it again!
Four to recover, and two to lie dead,
Two to putt out, making total Thirteen.
"How many, Colonel?"—Scratching his head,
"Eight—no, no, wait a bit—seven," he said.
Ev'n as he spoke,
Straightway an oak!
O, what a beautiful, beautiful tree!
Fifty-two feet,
Foliage complete—
And it grows on the edge of the Seventeenth Tee.

Stout Mrs. Y.,
Playing a tie,
Had a most difficult, difficult lie.

What's to be done?
Lift and lose one?
Clearly impossible—match to be won!
Far to the right
Chanc'd to catch sight
Of her rival, with back turn'd, addressing a shot—
Knew what to do;
Pointed a shoe;
And the ball trickled out to a *much* better spot.
O, Mrs. Y.,
Look at the sky!
See what a beautiful, beautiful pine!
With its far-spreading shade
What a *difference* it's made
To the look of the fairway of bare Number Nine!

But alas and alack!
It was eighteen months back
That the trees 'gan to spring this curious way.
Now our Golf Club is shut.
Not a drive or a putt,
Not a chip makes the echoes in P . . . . . .na today;
Not a Kroflite leaps now o'er those well-wooded lands—
But the Forest Department are rubbing their hands.

E. A. WODEHOUSE

The Ball and the Club

I shot a golf ball into the air;
It fell toward earth, I knew not where;
For who hath eye so strong and keen,
As to follow the flight of my ball to the green.

I lost a club I could not spare,
And searched for it most everywhere;
For who hath sight so keen and quick
As to trace the course of a missing stick.

Long, long afterwards, in an oak,
I found the golf ball still unbroke;
And the club—with a couple of nicks and a bend,
I found again in the bag of a friend.

FORBES LINDSAY

The City of Golf

Would you like to see a city given over,
Soul and body to a tyrannizing game?
If you would, there's little need to be a rover,
For St. Andrew's is the abject city's name.

It is surely quite superfluous to mention,
To a person who has been here half an hour,
That golf is what engrosses the attention
Of the people, with an all-absorbing power.

Rich and poor alike are smitten with the fever;
Their business and religion is to play;
And a man is scarcely deemed a true believer,
Unless he goes at least a round a day.

The city boasts an old and learned college,
Where you'd think the leading industry was Greek;
Even there the favoured instruments of knowledge
Are a driver and a putter and a cleek.

All the natives and the residents are patrons
Of this royal, ancient, irritating sport;
All the old men, all the young men, maids and matrons—
The universal populace, in short.

In the morning, when the feeble light grows stronger,
You may see the players going out in shoals;
And when night forbids their playing any longer,
They tell us how they did the different holes.

Golf, golf, golf—is all the story!
In despair my overburdened spirit sinks,
Till I wish that every golfer was in glory,
And I pray the sea may overflow the links.

One slender, struggling ray of consolation
Sustains me, very feeble though it be;
There are two who still escape infatuation,
My friend M'Foozle's one, the other's me.

As I write the words, M'Foozle enters blushing,
With a brassy and an iron in his hand . . .
This blow, so unexpected and so crushing,
Is more than I am able to withstand.

So now it but remains for me to die, sir.
Stay! There *is* another course I may pursue—
And perhaps upon the whole it would be wiser—
I will yield to fate and be a golfer too!

ROBERT FULLER MURRAY

One Down

Weight distributed,
  Free from strain,
Divot replaced,
  Familiar terrain,
Straight left arm,
  Unmoving head—
Here lies the golfer,
  Cold and dead.

RICHARD ARMOUR

Races and Contests

                    . . . let them
dig me a long pit for leaping. The spring in my
     knees is light.

                                        PINDAR

From the Greek Anthology

This torch, still burning in my hand,
Which I carried to victory,
Running swiftly in the sacred
Race of the young men,
A memorial of Prometheos
And the theft of fire,
I, Antiphanes,
The son of Antiphanes,
Dedicate to Hermes.

KRINAGORAS
Translated by Kenneth Rexroth

A Mighty Runner
(*Variation of a Greek Theme*)

The day when Charmus ran with five
In Arcady, as I'm alive,
He came in seventh.—"Five and one
Make seven, you say? It can't be done."—
Well, if you think it needs a note,
A friend in a fur overcoat
Ran with him, crying all the while,
"You'll beat 'em, Charmus, by a mile!"
And so he came in seventh.
Therefore, good Zoilus, you see
The thing is plain as plain can be;
And with four more for company,
He would have been eleventh.

EDWIN ARLINGTON ROBINSON

The Runner

On a flat road runs the well-train'd runner,
He is lean and sinewy with muscular legs,
He is thinly clothed, he leans forward as he runs,
With lightly closed fists and arms partially rais'd.

WALT WHITMAN

The Sprinters

The gun explodes them.
Pummeling, pistoning they fly
In time's face.
A go at the limit,
A terrible try
To smash the ticking glass,
Outpace the beat
That runs, that streaks away
Tireless, and faster than they.

Beside ourselves
(It is for us they run!)
We shout and pound the stands
For one to win
Loving him, whose hard
Grace-driven stride
Most mocks the clock
And almost breaks the bands
Which lock us in.

LEE MURCHISON

Runner

All visible, visibly
Moving things
Spin or swing,
One of the two,
Move as the limbs
Of a runner do,
To and fro,
Forward and back,
Or, as they swiftly
Carry him,
In orbit go
Round an endless track:
So, everywhere, every
Creature disporting
Itself according
To the Law of its making,
In the rivals' dance
Of a balanced pair
Or the ring-dance
Round a common centre,
Delights the eye
By its symmetry
As it changes place,
Blessing the unchangeable
Absolute rest
Of the space they share.

. . . .

The camera's eye
Does not lie,
But it cannot show
The life within,
The life of a runner
Or yours or mine,
That race which is neither
Fast nor slow
For nothing can ever
Happen twice,
That story which moves
Like music when
Begotten notes
New notes beget,
Making the flowing
Of time a growing,
Till what it could be
At last it is
Where fate is freedom,
Grace and surprise.

W. H. AUDEN

Notes on a Track Meet

Starter
If anyone has fun,
Why that's the starter with his gun—
The which he'd gladly aim
At the jumper of the same.

Century
The lad who runs the 100 yds.,
Accompanied by competing pds.,
Considers it a mighty ft.
If he is hot in every ht.—
But that is rarely on the cds.

15′ 1″
Who climbs the air on slender pole
Assumes a sudden stellar role;
But still he has to cross the bar,
Like Tennyson, to stay a star.

4:08 2/5
He wears the best of spikèd shoes,
And runs to win and not to lose,
And times his quarters on the dial
That measures two feet to the mile.

DAVID MC CORD

The Sluggard

Marcus, the sluggard, dreamed he ran a race,
and never went to sleep again in case—

LUCILIUS
Translated by Humbert Wolfe

Challenge

Leveling his pole like some quixotic lance,
trotting, trotting faster, faster to his mark,
slotting the pole, twisting upward to a bar,
contortioning clear, the vaulter drops in sand.

He wipes his hands and stumbles from the pit
with sand still sweated to his thighs and calves,
retrieves the pole and drags it like a mast
behind him down the cinder aisle, and waits.

I feel in my onlooker's hands the taped
and heavy barrel of the vaulter's pole
and see the bar notched higher for his leap.
His spikes clench earth, and all my muscles pull
to face a task with nothing but my skill
and struggle for the mark I must excel.

SAMUEL HAZO

58

Bicycalamity

There's panic in Paris.
C'est terrifique!
The six-day riders
Want a five-day week!

EDMUND W. PETERS

Pole Vault

He is running like a wasp,
Hanging on a long pole.
As a matter of course he floats in the sky,
Chasing the ascending horizon.
Now he has crossed the limit,
And pushed away his support.
For him there is nothing but a descent.
Oh, he falls helplessly.
Now on that runner, awkwardly fallen on the ground,
Once more
The horizon comes down,
Beating hard on his shoulders.

SHIRO MURANO
Translated from the Japanese by Satoru Sato
with the assistance of Constance Urdang

400-meter Freestyle

THE GUN full swing the swimmer catapults and cracks

$\qquad\qquad\qquad\qquad\qquad\qquad\qquad\qquad\quad$s

$\qquad\qquad\qquad\qquad\qquad\qquad\qquad\qquad\qquad$i

$\qquad\qquad\qquad\qquad\qquad\qquad\qquad\qquad\qquad\quad$x

feet away onto that perfect glass he catches at

a

n

$\quad$d

throws behind him scoop after scoop cunningly moving

$\qquad\qquad\qquad\qquad\qquad\qquad\qquad\qquad\qquad$t

$\qquad\qquad\qquad\qquad\qquad\qquad\qquad\qquad\qquad\quad$h

$\qquad\qquad\qquad\qquad\qquad\qquad\qquad\qquad\qquad\quad$e

water back to move him forward. Thrift is his wonderful

s

e

$\quad$c

ret; he has schooled out all extravagance. No muscle

$\qquad\qquad\qquad\qquad\qquad\qquad\qquad\qquad\qquad$r

$\qquad\qquad\qquad\qquad\qquad\qquad\qquad\qquad\qquad\quad$i

$\qquad\qquad\qquad\qquad\qquad\qquad\qquad\qquad\qquad\quad$p

ples without compensation wrist cock to heel snap to

h

$\;$i

$\quad$s

mobile mouth that siphons in the air that nurtures

$\qquad\qquad\qquad\qquad\qquad\qquad\qquad\qquad\qquad$h

$\qquad\qquad\qquad\qquad\qquad\qquad\qquad\qquad\qquad\quad$i

$\qquad\qquad\qquad\qquad\qquad\qquad\qquad\qquad\qquad\quad$m

at half an inch above sea level so to speak.

```
T
h
  e
astonishing  whites  of  the  soles  of  his  feet  rise
                                                a
                                                  n
                                                    d
salute  us  on  the  turns.  He  flips,  converts,  and  is  gone
a
l
  l
in  one.  We  watch  him  for  signs.  His  arms  are  steady  at
                                                  t
                                                    h
                                                      e
catch,  his  cadent  feet  tick  in  the  stretch,  they  know
t
h
  e
lesson  well.  Lungs  know,  too;  he  does  not  list  for
                                                a
                                                  i
                                                r
he  drives  along  on  little  sips  carefully  expended
b
u
  t
that  plum  red  heart  pumps  hard  cries  hurt  how  soon
                                                    i
                                                      t
                                                        s
near one more and makes its final surge     TIME: 4:25:9
```

MAXINE W. KUMIN

Eight Oars and a Coxswain

Eight oars compel
Our darting shell,
Eight oar-blades flash the sun;
The hard arms thrill,
The deep lungs fill,
Eight backs are bent as one.
All silver lined
We leave behind
Each wave of somber hue.
"Stroke! Stroke!
Stroke! Stroke!
Steady, Number Two!"

The sea-gulls go,
A drift of snow,
On Hudson's lights and shades;
The eagle swings
On splendid wings
Above the Palisades.
Let Caution steer
The shore anear,
But Valor takes the tide.
Stroke! Stroke!
"Stroke! Stroke!
Ease your forward slide!"

A fair league still
To old Cock Hill,
Where Spuyten Duyvil roars.

No time for play;
    Give 'way; give 'way!
And bend the driven oars!
    When breezes blow
    Then feather low
With level blades and true.
    "Stroke! Stroke!
    Stroke! Stroke!
Steady! Pull it thr-o-o-ough!"

ARTHUR GUITERMAN

Crew Cut

Now as the river fills with ice
The shells are locked up with the mice.
A world of shouts and grunts and groans
Has vanished with the megaphones.

DAVID MC CORD

The Boat Race

They are at their places, straining,
Arms stretched to the oars, waiting the word, and their chests
Heave, and their hearts are pumping fast; ambition
And nervousness take hold of them. The signal!
They shoot away; the noise goes up to the heavens,
The arms pull back to the chests, the water is churned
To a foam like snow; the start is very even,
The sea gapes open under the rush of the beaks
And the pull of the oars. The racers go no faster
When the chariots take the field, and the barrier springs
Cars into action, and the drivers lash
Whipping and shaking the reins. Applause and shouting
Volley and ring, and shrill excitement rises
From some with bets on the issue; all the woodland
Resounds, the shores are loud, and the beaten hillside
Sends back the uproar.

VIRGIL
from the Aeneid
Translated by Rolfe Humphries

Galway Races

It's there you'll see confectioners with sugar sticks and dainties,
The lozenges and oranges, lemonade and the raisins:
The gingerbread and spices to accommodate the ladies,
And a big crubeen for threepence to be picking while you're
    able.

It's there you'll see the gamblers, the thimbles and the garters,
And the sporting Wheel of Fortune with the four and twenty
        quarters.
There was others without scruple pelting wattles at poor
        Maggy,
And her father well contented and he looking at his daughter.

It's there you'll see the pipers and fiddlers competing,
And the nimble-footed dancers and they tripping on the
        daisies.
There was others crying segars and lights, and bills of all the
        races,
With the colour of the jockeys, the prize and horses' ages.

It's there you'd see the jockeys and they mounted on most
        stately,
The pink and blue, the red and green, the Emblem of our
        nation.
When the bell was rung for starting, the horses seemed
        impatient,
Though they never stood on ground, their speed was so
        amazing.

There was half a million people there of all denominations,
The Catholic, the Protestant, the Jew and Prespetarian.
There was yet no animosity, no matter what persuasion,
But *failte* and hospitality, inducing fresh acquaintance.

ANONYMOUS

failte: delight, greeting—L. M.

The Start

One to make ready
Two to get steady
And three to go.

OLD RHYME

Morning Workout

The sky unfolding its blankets to free
The morning.
Chill on the air. Clean odor of stables.
The grandstand green as the turf,
The pavilion flaunting its brilliance
For no one.
Beyond hurdles and hedges, swans, circling, cast
A contemplative radiance over the willow's shadows.
Day pales the toteboard lights,
Gilds the balls, heightens the stripes of the poles.
Dirt shines. White glisten of rails.
The track is bright as brine.
Their motion a flowing,
From prick of the ear to thick tail's shimmering drift,
The horses file forth.
Pink nostrils quiver, as who know they are showing their
    colors.
Ankles lift, as who hear without listening.
The bay, the brown, the chestnut, the roan have loaned
Their grace to the riders who rise in the stirrups, or hunch
Over the withers, gentling with mumbled song.
A mare ambles past, liquid eye askance.
Three, then four, canter by: voluptuous power
Pours through their muscles,
Dancing in pulse and nerve.
They glide in the stretch as on skis.
Two
Are put to a drive:
Centaur energy bounding as the dirt shudders, flies

Under the wuthering pace,
Hushes the hooves' thunders,
The body's unsyllabled eloquence rapidly
Dying away.
Dark-skinned stable-boys, as proud as kin
Of their display of vivacity, elegance,
Walk the racers back.
Foam laces the girths, sweaty haunches glow.
Slowly returning from the track, the horse is
Animal paradigm of innocence, discipline, force.
Blanketed, they go in.
Odor of earth
Enriches azuring air.

BABETTE DEUTSCH

The Chariot Race

Have you not seen them fighting for the lead,
Their chariots plunging when the barrier drops,
The drivers' surging hopes, the pounding fear
That drains exulting hearts? They close in,
Ply the lash, crouch over loosened reins,
The glowing axle spins, the drivers' bodies
Seem now to scrape the ground, and now to soar
Through empty air, wheels rising in the wind;
No hanging back, no rest: a golden cloud
Of sand swirls in their wake, the flecks of foam,
The breath of the pursuers, soak them through:
So great is their love for praise, their will to win.

VIRGIL
from the Georgics
Translated by Smith Palmer Bovie

The Closing of the Rodeo

The lariat snaps; the cowboy rolls
    His pack, and mounts and rides away.
Back to the land the cowboy goes.

Plumes of smoke from the factory sway
    In the setting sun. The curtain falls,
A train in the darkness pulls away.

Good-by, says the rain on the iron roofs.
    Good-by, say the barber poles.
Dark drum the vanishing horses' hooves.

WILLIAM JAY SMITH

Gallantly Within the Ring

Oh, it *is* LIFE! to see a proud
And dauntless man step, full of hopes,
Up to the P. C.* stakes and ropes,
Throw in his hat, and with a spring
Get gallantly within the ring;
Eye the wide crowd, and walk awhile,
Taking all cheerings with a smile:
To see him strip,—his well trained form,
White, glowing, muscular, and warm,
All beautiful in conscious power,
Relaxed and quiet, till the hour;
His glossy and transparent frame,
In radiant plight to strive for fame!
To look upon the clean shaped limb
In silk and flannel clothed trim;—
While round the waist the kerchief tied
Makes the flesh glow in richer pride.
'Tis more than LIFE,—to watch him hold
His hand forth, tremulous yet bold,
Over his second's, and to clasp
His rival's in a quiet grasp;
To watch the noble attitude
He takes,—the crowd in breathless mood;—
And then to see with adamant start,
The muscles set,—and the great heart
Hurl a courageous splendid light
Into the eye,—and then,—the FIGHT!

JOHN HAMILTON REYNOLDS
(1820)

* Pugilistic Club

Boxer

Poised, relaxed, as a cat that waits,
　　　　Too obviously bored, for the mouse to venture,
You endure the familiar ritual. They lace
　　　　The gloves on, lead you to the center,
The half-heard mutter and the touching hands.
　　　　The lights insist upon your thinning hair,

The best years are behind. Nothing at stake
　　　　Tonight; purse and crowd are small;
Only another fight among the hundred odd
　　　　Since boyhood and the animal
Tumblings in the street. Never a champion:
　　　　You fought him once, but lost the call;

And not again. These are the final years
　　　　As the ageing body threatens to rebel
And they send the upstart boys to take you.
　　　　One will. But not tonight. The bell
Calls you to work, and to your finest night.
　　　　The crowd held silent by your fluent spell,

For once not screaming for the knockout punch
　　　　You never had, watches an adept in an art
That, like an actor's, lives in the splendid moment
　　　　And the betraying memory. You dart
The left hand like a bird that, roused to danger,
　　　　Rakes at the hunter's eyes, and start

The young blood flowing as the right hand pounds
    The ribs and belly and you move away,
Then in, tense and pure and timeless
    In your perfect dance. Coolly you display
The repertoire of moves and punches mastered
    Through the dull years of sweat for pay.

You win. Time, masked as this beaten boy,
    Has his hand shaken and his matted hair
Ruffled by your glove. You shower, dress,
    Quietly collect your winner's share,
And leave, a tired workman going home,
    Who carved a marble image on the air.

JOSEPH P. CLANCY

The Fancy

(WITH A BOW TO GEORGE BORROW's *Lavengro*)

The bruisers of England, the men of tremendous renown,
The choice of the Fancy who tooled through the dust from the
      Town
With peers in their chariots all hasting toward glory and fame,
And gigs and blood horses that raced till they came to the
      game—

Their times and their seasons, their glory, alas, that must pass
With the turf-treading masters, to fade like the flower of the
      grass!

Cribb, champion of England, the lion-faced, leading the van;
And Belcher the Younger, a most scientifical man;
The savage, dark Shelton whose blow was a thunderbolt dealt,
The tiny and terrible Randall, the man-eating Celt—

The luck of the ring and the roaring of mass and of class
To the rush and the rally and shifting of feet on the grass!

Black Richmond; the Welshman; and Hudson the Bulldog, and
      Tom—
That tall Tom of Bedford, brown-eyed, of a thunderous calm,
That yeoman of Holborn, fit follower of Broughton and Brain
Whose portraits grinned down, in his pub, on the hubbub
      profane—

The clamor of backers in bars and the clinking of glass
At a name new to fame, soon to pass like a cloud from the grass!

Straight left and Long Melford; the battlers stripped down to
    the buff;
The blows of bare morleys, and neither to hollo enough;
The swells with their whiskers, their beavers aslant on the ear,
In greatcoat and hessians, to parley and wager and peer—

The cross and the counter, the feint and the grunt and the
    thud;
The down's sun and shadow; the challenger first drawing
    blood!

The days of the Fancy! A turbulent tale and a dream
That feats of fair field and no favor are fain to redeem
In old colored prints; the profession that Borrow extolled
As though he were Homer invoking the heroes of old—

Their life in his language; his memory never to pass
Though faded their glory as fadeth the flower of the grass!

WILLIAM ROSE BENÉT

The Nonpareil's Grave

Far out in the wilds of Oregon,
  On a lonely mountain side,
Where Columbia's mighty waters
  Roll down to the ocean side;
Where the giant fir and cedar
  Are imaged in the wave,
O'ergrown with firs and lichens,
  I found Jack Dempsey's grave.

I found no marble monolith,
  No broken shaft, or stone,
Recording sixty victories,
  This vanquished victor won;
No rose, no shamrock could I find
  No mortal here to tell
Where sleeps in this forsaken spot
  Immortal Nonpareil.

A winding wooden canyon road
  That mortals seldom tread,
Leads up this lonely mountain,
  To the desert of the dead.
And the Western sun was sinking
  In Pacific's golden wave,
And those solemn pines kept watching,
  Over poor Jack Dempsey's grave.

Forgotten by ten thousand throats,
  That thundered his acclaim,
Forgotten by his friends and foes,
  Who cheered his very name.
Oblivion wraps his faded form,
  But ages hence shall save
The memory of that Irish lad
  That fills poor Dempsey's grave.

Oh, Fame, why sleeps thy favored son
  In wilds, in woods, in weeds,
And shall he ever thus sleep on,
  Interred his valiant deeds?
'Tis strange New York should thus forget
  Its "bravest of the brave"
And in the fields of Oregon,
  Unmarked, leave Dempsey's grave.

M. J. MC MAHON

Jack Dempsey the Nonpareil, a Brooklyn boy, was a middleweight champion of the late 19th century, noted for his gameness. He died young.
The poem was first printed anonymously in the *Portland Oregonian*, De-
cember 10, 1899. As a result of it, his friends raised money for a tomb-
stone, and the poem now appears on it.—L. M.

The Boxing Match

They take their stand, each rising
On the balls of his feet, their arms upraised, and rolling
Their heads back from the punch. They spar, they lead,
They watch for openings. Dares, much the younger,
Is much the better in footwork; old Entellus
Has to rely on strength; his knees are shaky,
His wind not what it was. They throw their punches,
And many miss; and some, with a solid thump,
Land on the ribs or chest; temples and ears
Feel the wind of a miss, or the jaws rattle
When a punch lands. Entellus stands flat-footed,
Wasting no motion, just a slip of the body,
The watchful eyes alert. And Dares, feinting,
Like one who artfully attacks a city,
Tries this approach, then that, dancing around him
In varied vain attack. Entellus, rising,
Draws back his right (in fact, he telegraphs it),
And Dares, seeing it coming, slips aside;
Entellus lands on nothing but the wind
And, thrown off balance, heavily comes down
Flat on his face, as falls on Erymanthus
A thunder-smitten oak, and so on, and so on.
Roaring, the Trojans and Sicilians both
Rise to their feet; the noise goes up to heaven;
Acestes rushes in, to raise his comrade
In pity and sorrow. But that old-time fighter
Is not slowed down a bit, nor made more wary;
His rage is terrible, and his shame awakens
A consciousness of strength. He chases Dares

All over the ring, left, right, left, right, the punches
Rattle like hailstones on a roof; he batters Dares,
Spins him halfway around with one hand, clouts him
Straight with the other again. At last Aeneas
Steps in and stops it, with a word of comfort
For the exhausted Dares.

VIRGIL
from the Aeneid
Translated by Rolfe Humphries

The Boxer's Face

Olympicus, don't look into a mirror
lest, like Narcissus, you drown yourself—in terror.

LUCILIUS
Translated by Humbert Wolfe

79

On Hurricane Jackson

Now his nose's bridge is broken, one eye
will not focus and the other is astray;
trainers whisper in his mouth while one ear
listens to itself, clenched like a fist;
generally shadow-boxing in a smoky room,
his mind hides like the aching boys
who lost a contest in the Pan-Hellenic games
and had to take the back roads home,
but someone else, his perfect youth,
laureled in newsprint and dollar bills,
triumphs forever on the great white way
to the statistical Sparta of the champs.

ALAN DUGAN

Wrestlers

With collars be they yoked, to prove the arm at length,
Like bulls set head to head, with meere delyver strength,
Or by the girdles graspt, they practice with the hip,
The forward, backward, falx, the mare, the turn, the trip;
When stript into their shirts, each other they invade
Within a spacious ring, by the beholders made,
According to the law.

> MICHAEL DRAYTON
> *from* Poly-olbion
> (1613)

meere delyver: more nimble
falx: a crouch
mare: a throw in wrestling,
   e.g., the flying mare—L. M.

The World's Worst Boxer

Apis! the men you boxed with, grateful that you
never hit one of them, erect this statue.

> LUCILIUS
> Translated by Humbert Wolfe

Pleasures of the Country

When we please to walk abroad
   For our recreation,
In the fields is our abode,
   Full of delectation.

IZAAK WALTON

Walking

To walk abroad is, not with eyes,
But thoughts, the fields to see and prize;
   Else may the silent feet,
     Like logs of wood,
Move up and down, and see no good,
   Nor joy nor glory meet.

Ev'n carts and wheels their place do change,
But cannot see; though very strange
   The glory that is by:
     Dead puppets may
Move in the bright and glorious day,
   Yet not behold the sky.

And are not men than they more blind,
Who having eyes yet never find
   The bliss in which they move:
     Like statues dead
They up and down are carried,
   Yet neither see nor love. . . .

To walk is by a thought to go,
To move in spirit to and fro,
   To mind the good we see;
     To taste the sweet;
Observing all the things we meet
   How choice and rich they be.

To note the beauty of the day,
And golden fields of corn survey;
   Admire each pretty flower
     With its sweet smell;
To praise their Maker, and to tell
   The marks of His great power.

To fly abroad like active bees,
Among the hedges and the trees,
   To cull the dew that lies
     On every blade,
From every blossom, till we lade
   Our minds, as they their thighs.

Observe those rich and glorious things,
The rivers, meadows, woods, and springs,
   The fructifying sun;
     To note from far
The rising of each twinkling star
   For us his race to run.

A little child these well perceives,
Who, tumbling in green grass and leaves,
   May rich as kings be thought.
     But there's a sight
Which perfect manhood may delight,
   To which we shall be brought.

While in those pleasant paths we talk
'Tis that towards which at last we walk;
   For we may by degrees
     Wisely proceed
Pleasures of love and praise to heed,
   From viewing herbs and trees.

THOMAS TRAHERNE
(1637?–1674)

The Hike

Clear and high, a mountain.
And my heart sinks
out of custom, but I try
because I am with you.

We keep on going
on a gradual incline
until thighs tingle
and a shiver's in the spine;

mount steadily,
taking joy from a difficulty,
each thrust ahead
accomplished mutely—

and approach the top
moving so deliberately,
breath for shortened breath,
each step's a splendid agony.

But now the mind shines,
sweat freezes, and we
unclasp our hands—the
mountain shakes us very gently.

NEIL WEISS

The Walk

He walked through the woods
and saw the merging
of the tall trunks
in the green distance,—
the undergrowth
of mottled green,
with sunlight and shadow,
and flowers starting

here and there
on the mottled ground;
he looked along
the green distance
and up towards
the greenly-laden
curving boughs
of the tall trees;

and down a slope
as he walked onward
down the sloping
ground, he saw
in among
the green, broken,
the blue shimmering
of lake-water.

W. W. EUSTACE ROSS

Climbing in Glencoe

The sun became a small round moon
And the scared rocks grew pale and weak
As mist surged up the col, and soon
So thickly everywhere it tossed
That though I reached the peak
With height and depth both lost
It might as well have been a plain;
Yet when, groping my way again,
On to the scree I stept
It went with me, and as I swept
Down its loose rumbling course
Balanced I rode it like a circus horse.

ANDREW YOUNG

To Walk on Hills

To walk on hills is to employ legs
As porters of the head and heart
Jointly adventuring towards
Perhaps true equanimity.

To walk on hills is to see sights
And hear sounds unfamiliar.
When in wind the pine-tree roars,
When crags with bleating echo,
When water foams below the fall,
Heart records that journey
As memorable indeed;
Head reserves opinion,
Confused by the wind.

A view of three shires and the sea!
Seldom so much at once appears
Of the coloured world, says heart.
Head is glum, says nothing.

Legs become weary, halting
To sprawl in a rock's shelter,
While the sun drowsily blinks
On head at last brought low—
This giddied passenger of legs
That has no word to utter.

Heart does double duty,
As heart, and as head,
With portentous trifling.
A castle, on its crag perched,
Across the miles between is viewed
With awe as across years.

Now a daisy pleases,
Pleases and astounds, even,
That on a garden lawn could blow
All summer long with no esteem.

And the buzzard's horrid poise,
And the plover's misery,
And the important beetle's
Blue-green-shiny back. . . .

To walk on hills is to employ legs
To march away and lose the day.
Confess, have you known shepherds?
And are they not a witless race,
Prone to quaint visions?
Not thus from solitude
(Solitude sobers only)
But from long hilltop striding.

ROBERT GRAVES

The Mountains

The mountains? Rising from some wet ravine,
After a night impaled on evergreen,
The hiker crawls up ledges and down ridges,
Pursued by flies, mosquitos, gnats, and midges,
Until, sore-footed, and sore-headed too,
He scales a rockface and admires the view—
Far off, below, a city on the plain.
Oh how he wishes he were there again!

WALKER GIBSON

High Brow

He climbed up the peak
To the manner born,
And claimed it was mind
Over Matterhorn.

ROBERT FITCH

In the Mountains on a Summer Day

Gently I stir a white feather fan,
With open shirt sitting in a green wood.
I take off my cap and hang it on a jutting stone;
A wind from the pine-trees trickles on my bare head.

LI PO
Translated by Arthur Waley

Having Climbed to the Topmost Peak
of the Incense-Burner Mountain

Up and up, the Incense-burner Peak!
In my heart is stored what my eyes and ears perceived.
All the year—detained by official business;
To-day at last I got a chance to go.
Grasping the creepers, I clung to dangerous rocks;
My hands and feet—weary with groping for hold.
There came with me three or four friends,
But two friends dared not go further.
At last we reached the topmost crest of the Peak;
My eyes were blinded, my soul rocked and reeled.
The chasm beneath me—ten thousand feet;
The ground I stood on, only a foot wide.
If you have not exhausted the scope of seeing and hearing,
How can you realize the wideness of the world?
The waters of the River looked narrow as a ribbon,
P'ēn Castle smaller than a man's fist.
How it clings, the dust of the world's halter!
It chokes my limbs: I cannot shake it away.
Thinking of retirement, I heaved an envious sigh,
Then, with lowered head, came back to the Ants' Nest.

PO CHÜ-I
Translated by Arthur Waley

On Middleton Edge

If this life-saving rock should fail
Yielding too much to my embrace
And rock and I to death should race,
The rock would stay there in the dale
While I, breaking my fall,
Would still go on
Farther than any wandering star has gone.

ANDREW YOUNG

Of Swimming in Lakes and Rivers

In the pale summertime, when far above you
In only the largest trees the winds are sighing,
You must float inert in a pool or in a river
Like the waterweeds in which pike are lying.
Your flesh grows light in water. Thrust your arm
Softly from water into air and now
The little wind cradles it forgetfully,
Seeming to take it for a brown bough.

At midday the sky proffers a great stillness.
You close your eyes when the swallows pass you.
The mud is warm. When the cool bubbles rise up
You know that a fish has just swum across you.
Your body, your thigh and motionless arm
Lie in quiet unity, only when the cool
Fish are swimming lazily across you
Can you feel the sun shine down upon the pool.

In the evening when, from long lying,
You grow so lazy that all your limbs prickle
Without a backward glance you must fling yourself,
Splashing, into a blue river where the rapids ripple.
It is best to hold out until evening comes
For then, like a shark over stream and shrubbery,
The pale sky looms, angry and gluttonous,
And all things are just as they should be.

You must, of course, lie on your back quietly
As is usual and let yourself go on drifting.
You must not swim, no, but only act as if
You were a mass of flotsam slowly shifting.
You must look up at the sky and act as if
A woman carried you, and it is so.
Quiet, without disturbance, as the good God himself does
When at evening he swims in his rivers here below.

BERTOLT BRECHT
Translated by H. R. Hays

The Swimmer

In dog-days plowmen quit their toil,
And frog-ponds in the meadow boil,
And grasses on the upland broil,
And all the coiling things uncoil,
And eggs and meats and Christians spoil.

A mile away the valley breaks
(So all good valleys do) and makes
A cool green water for hot heads' sakes,
And sundry sullen dog-days' aches.

The swimmer's body is white and clean,
It is washed by a water of deepest green
The color of leaves in a starlight scene,
And it is as white as the stars between.

But the swimmer's soul is a thing possessed,
His soul is naked as his breast,
Remembers not its east and west,
And ponders this way, I have guessed:

I have no home in the cruel heat
On alien soil that blisters feet.
This water is my native seat,
And more than ever cool and sweet,
So long by forfeiture escheat.

O my forgiving element!
I gash you to my heart's content

And never need be penitent,
So light you float me when breath is spent
And close again where my rude way went.

And now you close above my head,
And I lie low in a soft green bed
That dog-days never have visited.
"By the sweat of thy face shalt thou eat bread:"
The garden's curse is at last unsaid.

What do I need of senses five?
Why eat, or drink, or sweat, or wive?
What do we strive for when we strive?
What do we live for when alive?

And what if I do not rise again,
Never to goad a heated brain
To hotter excesses of joy and pain?
Why should it be against the grain
To lie so cold and still and sane?

Water-bugs play shimmer-shimmer,
Naked body's just a glimmer,
Watch ticks every second grimmer:
Come to the top, O wicked swimmer!

JOHN CROWE RANSOM

From The Angler's Song

As inward love breeds outward talk,
The hound some praise, and some the hawk,
Some, better pleas'd with private sport,
Use tennis, some a mistress court:
    But these delights I neither wish,
    Nor envy, while I freely fish.

Who hunts doth oft in danger ride;
Who hawks, lures oft both far and wide
Who uses games shall often prove
A loser; but who falls in love,
    Is fetter'd in fond Cupid's snare:
    My angle breeds me no such care.

Of recreation there is none
So free as fishing is alone;
All other pastimes do no less
Than mind and body both possess:
    My hand alone my work can do,
    So I can fish and study too.

I care not, I, to fish in seas,
Fresh rivers best my mind do please,
Whose sweet calm course I contemplate,
And seek in life to imitate:
    In civil bounds I fain would keep,
    And for my past offences weep.

And when the timorous Trout I wait
To take, and he devours my bait,
How poor a thing, sometimes I find,
Will captivate a greedy mind:
     And when none bite, I praise the wise
     Whom vain allurements ne'er surprise.

But yet, though while I fish, I fast,
I make good fortune my repast;
And thereunto my friend invite,
In whom I more than that delight:
     Who is more welcome to my dish
     Than to my angle was my fish.

W. B.
(Izaak Walton)

The Pike

I take it he doesn't think at all,
But muscles his slippery fight, an engine
Green deep, powering his belly flash
In his water mother, his horizonless well;
The hooked gill the fault in the world
Of his will, his preying paradise.

Near enough to net I have him,
And the murk of his body is my fear
Of our meeting somehow equally.
He pauses on the strain of my line;
I have him netted, sluicing the air,
How pure brave my wet thrasher, my enemy.

JOHN BRUCE

The Last Chance

Within the streams, Pausanias saith,
    That down Cocytus valley flow,
Girdling the grey domain of Death,
    The spectral fishes come and go;
The ghosts of trout flit to and fro.
    Persephone, fulfil my wish;
And grant that in the shades below
    My ghost may land the ghosts of fish.

ANDREW LANG

Fly-Fishing

I never wander where the bord'ring reeds
O'erlook the muddy stream, whose tangling weeds
Perplex the fisher; I, nor choose to bear
The thievish nightly net, nor barbed spear;
Nor drain I ponds the golden carp to take,
Nor troll for pikes, dispeoplers of the lake.
Around the steel no tortured worm shall twine,
No blood of living insect stain my line;
Let me, less cruel, cast the feathered hook,
With pliant rod athwart the pebbled brook,
Silent along the mazy margin stray,
And with the fur-wrought fly delude the prey.

JOHN GAY
from Rural Sports
(1720)

Fishing

We were a noisy crew; the sun in heaven
Beheld not vales more beautiful than ours;
Nor saw a band in happiness and joy
Richer, or worthier of the ground they trod.
I could record with no reluctant voice
The woods of autumn, and their hazel bowers
With milk-white clusters hung; the rod and line,
True symbol of hope's foolishness, whose strong
And unreproved enchantment led us on
By rocks and pools shut out from every star,
All the green summer, to forlorn cascades
Among the windings hid of mountain brooks.

WILLIAM WORDSWORTH
from The Prelude

Salmon-Fishing

The days shorten, the south blows wide for showers now,
The south wind shouts to the rivers,
The rivers open their mouths and the salt salmon
Race up into the freshet.
In Christmas month against the smoulder and menace
Of a long angry sundown
Red ash of the dark solstice, you see the anglers,
Pitiful, cruel, primeval,
Like the priests of the people that built Stonehenge,
Dark silent forms, performing
Remote solemnities in the red shallows
Of the river's mouth at the year's turn,
Drawing landward their live bullion, the bloody mouths
And scales full of the sunset
Twitch on the rocks, no more to wander at will
The wild Pacific pasture nor wanton and spawning
Race up into fresh water.

ROBINSON JEFFERS

The Careful Angler

The careful angler chose his nook
At morning by the lilied brook,
And all the noon his rod he plied
By that romantic riverside.
Soon as the evening hours decline
Tranquilly he'll return to dine,
And, breathing forth a pious wish,
Will cram his belly full of fish.

ROBERT LOUIS STEVENSON

A Green Stream

I have come on the River of Yellow Flowers,
Borne by the current of a green stream
Rounding ten thousand turns through the mountains
To journey less than a hundred li.
Rapids hum on scattered stones,
Light is dim in the close pines,
The surface of an inlet sways with nut-horns,
Weeds are lush along the banks.
Down in my heart I have always been clear
As this clarity of waters.
Oh, to remain on a broad flat rock
And cast my fishing-line forever!

WANG WÊI
Translated by Witter Bynner
and Kiang Kang-hu

And Angling, Too

And angling, too, that solitary vice,
Whatever Izaak Walton sings or says:
The quaint, old, cruel coxcomb, in his gullet
Should have a hook, and a small trout to pull it.

LORD BYRON
from Don Juan

How They Bite

Wind from the south, hook in the mouth.
Wind from the east, bite the least.
Wind from the north, further off.
Wind from the west, bite the best.

OLD RHYME

The Old Squire

I like the hunting of the hare
    Better than that of the fox;
I like the joyous morning air,
    And the crowing of the cocks.

I like the calm of the early fields,
    The ducks asleep by the lake,
The quiet hour which Nature yields,
    Before mankind is awake.

I like the pheasants and feeding things
    Of the unsuspicious morn;
I like the flap of the wood-pigeon's wings
    As she rises from the corn.

I like the blackbird's shriek, and his rush
    From the turnips as I pass by,
And the partridge hiding her head in a bush
    For her young ones cannot fly.

I like those things, and I like to ride
    When all the world is in bed,
To the top of the hill where the sky grows wide,
    And where the sun grows red.

The beagles at my horse heels trot
    In silence after me;
There's Ruby, Roger, Diamond, Dot,
    Old Slut and Margery,

A score of names well used, and dear,
    The names my childhood knew;
The horn, with which I rouse their cheer,
    Is the horn my father blew.

I like the hunting of the hare
    Better than that of the fox;
The new world still is all less fair
    Than the old world it mocks.

I covet not a wider range
    Than these dear manors give;
I take my pleasures without change,
    And as I lived I live.

I leave my neighbours to their thought;
    My choice it is, and pride,
On my own lands to find my sport,
    In my own fields to ride.

The hare herself no better loves
    The field where she was bred,
Than I the habit of these groves,
    My own inherited.

I know my quarries every one,
    The meuse where she sits low;
The road she chose to-day was run
    A hundred years ago.

The lags, the gills, the forest ways,
    The hedgerows one and all,

These are the kingdoms of my chase,
  And bounded by my wall;

Nor has the world a better thing,
  Though one should search it round,
Than thus to live one's own sole king,
  Upon one's own sole ground.

I like the hunting of the hare;
  It brings me, day by day,
The memory of old days as fair,
  With dead men past away.

To these, as homeward still I ply
  And pass the churchyard gate
Where all are laid as I must lie,
  I stop and raise my hat.

I like the hunting of the hare;
  New sports I hold in scorn.
I like to be as my fathers were,
  In the days ere I was born.

WILFRID SCAWEN BLUNT

John Peel

D'ye ken John Peel with his coat so gray?
D'ye ken John Peel at the break of the day?
D'ye ken John Peel when he's far, far away,
With his hounds and his horn in the morning?
   'Twas the sound of his horn called me from my bed,
   And the cry of his hounds has me oft-times led,
   For Peel's *View-hollo* would waken the dead,
   Or a fox from his lair in the morning.

D'ye ken that bitch whose tongue is death?
D'ye ken her sons of peerless faith?
D'ye ken that a fox with his last breath
Cursed them all as he died in the morning?

Yes, I ken John Peel and Ruby too
Ranter and Royal and Bellman as true;
From the drag to the chase, from the chase to a view,
From a view to the death in the morning.

And I've followed John Peel both often and far
O'er the rasper-fence and the gate and the bar,
From Low Denton Holme up to Scratchmere Scar,
When we vied for the brush in the morning.

Then here's to John Peel with my heart and soul,
Come fill—fill to him another strong bowl:
And we'll follow John Peel through fair and through foul,
While we're waked by his horn in the morning.

'Twas the sound of his horn called me from my bed,
And the cry of his hounds has me oft-times led,
For Peel's *View-hollo* would waken the dead
Or a fox from his lair in the morning.

JOHN WOODCOCK GRAVES

Horse & Rider

The rider
Is fat
As that (   )
Or wider (   )
In torso
Of course
The horse
Is more so (   )

WEY ROBINSON

Old Blue

I had a dog and his name was Blue,
And I betcha five dollars he's a good dog too.
Saying, "Come on Blue, mm mm."

Shouldered my axe and I tooted my horn,
Gonna get me a possum in the new-ground corn.
"Go on, Blue, I'm comin' too."

Chased that possum up a 'simmon tree;
Blue looked at the possum, possum looked at me,
Saying, "Go on, Blue, you can have some too."

Baked that possum good and brown,
Laid them sweet potatoes 'round and 'round,
Saying, "Come on, Blue, you can have some too."

"Blue, what makes your eyes so red?"
"I've run them possums till I'm almost dead."
"Go on, Blue, I'm comin' too."

Old Blue died, and he died so hard
That he jarred the ground in my backyard,
Saying, "Go on, Blue, I'm comin' too."

I dug his grave with a silver spade,
And I let him down with a golden chain,
Saying, "Go on, Blue, I'm comin' too."

When I get to Heaven, first thing I'll do,
Grab my horn, and I'll blow for old Blue.
Saying, "Come on, Blue, finally got here too."

ANONYMOUS

The Friar

Though I be now a grey, grey friar,
Yet I was once a hale young knight;
The cry of my dogs was the only choir
In which my spirit did take delight.

THOMAS LOVE PEACOCK
from Maid Marian

Beagles

Over rock and wrinkled ground
Ran the lingering nose of hound,
The little and elastic hare
Stretched herself nor stayed to stare.

Stretched herself, and far away
Darted through the chinks of day,
Behind her, shouting out her name,
The whole blind world galloping came.

Over hills a running line
Curled like a whip-lash, fast and fine,
Past me sailed the sudden pack
Along the taut and tingling track.

From the far flat scene each shout
Like jig-saw piece came tumbling out,
I took and put them all together,
And then they turned into a tether.

A tether that held me to the hare
Here, there, and everywhere.

W. R. RODGERS

My Heart's in the Highlands

My heart's in the Highlands, my heart is not here;
My heart's in the Highlands a-chasing the deer;
A-chasing the wild deer, and following the roe,
My heart's in the Highlands wherever I go.
Farewell to the Highlands, farewell to the North,
The birth-place of valor, the country of worth;
Wherever I wander, wherever I rove,
The hills of the Highlands forever I love.

Farewell to the mountains high-covered with snow;
Farewell to the straths and green valleys below;
Farewell to the forests and wild-hanging woods;
Farewell to the torrents and loud-pouring floods.
My heart's in the Highlands, my heart is not here;
My heart's in the Highlands a-chasing the deer;
A-chasing the wild deer, and following the roe,
My heart's in the Highlands, wherever I go.

ROBERT BURNS

The Lincolnshire Poacher

When I was bound apprentice, in famous Lincolnshire,
Full well I serv'd my master for more than seven year,
Till I took up to poaching, as you shall quickly hear;
Oh, 'tis my delight on a shining night in the season of the year.

As me and my companions were setting of a snare,
'Twas then we spied the game-keeper, for him we did not care,
For we can wrestle and fight, my boys, and jump o'er anywhere.
Oh, 'tis my delight on a shining night in the season of the year.

As me and my companions were setting four or five,
And, taking on 'em up again, we caught a hare alive,
We took the hare alive, my boys, and through the woods did
        steer.
Oh, 'tis my delight on a shining night in the season of the year.

I threw him on my shoulder, and then we trudged home,
We took him to a neighbour's house and sold him for a crown,
We sold him for a crown, my boys, but I did not tell you where.
Oh, 'tis my delight on a shining night in the season of the year.

Success to ev'ry gentleman that lives in Lincolnshire,
Success to ev'ry poacher that wants to sell a hare,
Bad luck to ev'ry game-keeper that will not sell his deer.
Oh, 'tis my delight on a shining night in the season of the year.

ANONYMOUS

Hawking

When making for the brook, the falconer doth espy
On river, plash, or mere, where store of fowl doth lie,
Whence forced over land, by skillful falconers trade,
A fair convenient flight may easily be made.
He whistleth off his hawks, whose nimble pinions straight
Do work themselves by turns into a stately height,
And if that after check, the one or both do go,
Sometimes he them the lure, sometimes doth water show.
The trembling fowl that hear the jigging hawk-bells ring
And find it is too late to trust then to their wing,
Lie flat upon the flood, whilst the high-mounted hawks,
Then being lords alone in their ethereal walks,
Aloft so bravely stir, their bells so thick that shake,
Which when the falconer sees, that scarce one plane they make,
The gallantest birds, saith he, that ever flew on wing
And swears there is a flight were worthy of a King.
    Then making to the flood to force the fowls to rise,
The fierce and eager hawks, down thrilling from the skies,
Make sundry canceleers e'er they the fowl can reach,
Which then to save their lives, their wings do lively stretch.
But when the whizzing bells the silent air do cleave
And that their greatest speed them vainly do deceive,
And the sharp, cruel hawks they at their backs do view,
Themselves for very fear they instantly ineawe.
    The hawks get up again into their former place
And ranging here and there in that their airy race;
Still as the fearfull fowl attempt to scape away,
With many a stooping brave, them in again they lay.
But when the falconers take their hawking-poles in hand,

And crossing of the brook, do put it over land,
The hawk gives it a souse that makes it to rebound
Well near the height of man, sometime above the ground,
Oft takes a leg, or wing, oft takes away the head,
And oft from neck to tail, the back in two doth shred.
With many a wo ho ho and jocond lure again,
When he his quarry makes upon the grassy plain.

MICHAEL DRAYTON
from Poly-olbion
(1613)

September

And in September, O what keen delight!
  Falcons and astors, merlins, sparrowhawks;
  Decoy-birds that shall lure your game in flocks;
And hounds with bells; and gauntlets stout and tight;
Wide pouches; crossbows shooting out of sight;
  Arblasts and javelins; balls and ball-cases;
  All birds the best to fly at; moulting these,
Those reared by hand; with finches mean and slight;
And for their chase, all birds the best to fly;
  And each to each of you be lavish still
    In gifts; and robbery find no gainsaying;
And if you meet with travelers going by,
  Their purses from your purse's flow shall fill;
  And avarice be the only outcast thing.

FOLGORE DA SAN GEMINIANO
(13th century)
Translated by Dante Gabriel Rossetti

A Runnable Stag

When the pods went pop on the broom, green broom,
  And apples began to be golden-skinned,
We harboured a stag in the Priory coomb,
  And we feathered his trail up-wind, up-wind,
  We feathered his trail up-wind—
    A stag of warrant, a stag, a stag,
    A runnable stag, a kingly crop,
    Brow, bay and tray and three on top,
    A stag, a runnable stag.

Then the huntsman's horn rang yap, yap, yap,
  And "Forwards" we heard the harbourer shout;
But 'twas only a brocket that broke a gap
  In the beechen underwood, driven out,
  From the underwood, antlered out
    By warrant and might of the stag, the stag,
    The runnable stag, whose lordly mind
    Was bent on sleep, though beamed and tined
    He stood, a runnable stag.

So we tufted the covert till afternoon
  With Tinkerman's Pup and Bell-of-the-North;
And hunters were sulky and hounds out of tune
  Before we tufted the right stag forth,
  Before we tufted him forth,
    The stag of warrant, the wily stag,
    The runnable stag with his kingly crop,
    Brow, bay and tray and three on top,
    The royal and runnable stag.

It was Bell-of-the-North and Tinkerman's Pup
   That stuck to the scent till the copse was drawn.
"Tally ho! tally ho!" and the hunt was up,
   The tufters whipped and the pack laid on,
   The resolute pack laid on,
      And the stag of warrant away at last,
      The runnable stag, the same, the same,
      His hoofs on fire, his horns like flame,
      A stag, a runnable stag.

"Let your gelding be: if you check or chide
   He stumbles at once and you're out of the hunt;
For three hundred gentlemen, able to ride,
   On hunters accustomed to bear the brunt,
   Accustomed to bear the brunt,
      Are after the runnable stag, the stag,
      The runnable stag with his kingly crop,
      Brow, bay and tray and three on top,
      The right, the runnable stag."

By perilous paths in coomb and dell,
   The heather, the rocks, and the river-bed,
The pace grew hot, for the scent lay well,
   And a runnable stag goes right ahead,
   The quarry went right ahead—
      Ahead, ahead, and fast and far;
      His antlered crest, his cloven hoof,
      Brow, bay and tray and three aloof,
      The stag, the runnable stag.

For a matter of twenty miles and more,
   By the densest hedge and the highest wall,

Through herds of bullocks he baffled the lore
  Of harbourer, huntsman, hounds and all,
  Of harbourer, hounds, and all—
    The stag of warrant, the wily stag,
    For twenty miles, and five and five,
    He ran, and he never was caught alive,
    This stag, this runnable stag.

When he turned at bay in the leafy gloom,
  In the emerald gloom where the brook ran deep,
He heard in the distance the rollers boom,
  And he saw in a vision of peaceful sleep,
  In a wonderful vision of sleep,
    A stag of warrant, a stag, a stag,
    A runnable stag in a jewelled bed,
    Under the sheltering ocean dead,
    A stag, a runnable stag.

So a fateful hope lit up his eye,
  And he opened his nostrils wide again,
And he tossed his branching antlers high
  As he headed the hunt down the Charlock glen
  As he raced down the echoing glen—
    For five miles more, the stag, the stag,
    For twenty miles, and five and five,
    Not to be caught now, dead or alive,
    The stag, the runnable stag.

Three hundred gentlemen, able to ride,
  Three hundred horses as gallant and free,
Beheld him escape on the evening tide,
  Far out till he sank in the Severn Sea,

Till he sank in the depths of the sea—
The stag, the buoyant stag, the stag
That slept at last in a jewelled bed
Under the sheltering ocean spread,
The stag, the runnable stag.

JOHN DAVIDSON

The Hunter

The hunter crouches in his blind
'Neath camouflage of every kind,
And conjures up a quacking noise
To lend allure to his decoys.
This grown-up man, with pluck and luck,
Is hoping to outwit a duck.

OGDEN NASH

Contest

Back from the kill
They sat drinking tea,
Studying Audubon.
I, the eccentric neighbor,
Said no, I'd rather not see
The pheasant,
Or admire the woodcocks.
I gave no lecture
Praised the brew
And was generally pleasant.
Still, when someone suggested
That fresh air might be good for me
I made it clear
This was no gossamer poet here
But a former first-baseman
Hiker-in-the-woods
And recent rock-thrower.
Bragging proceeded to exercises
And of three girls, I clearly was best.
Having antagonized everyone
(Except the silent male cleaning his gun)
I went home
Not murderer,
Just winner.

FLORENCE VICTOR

The Joys of Locomotion

Row, row, row your boat
Gently down the stream,
Merrily, merrily, merrily, merrily
Life is but a dream.

OLD SONG

Morning on the Lièvre

Far above us where a jay
Screams his matins to the day,
Capped with gold and amethyst,
Like a vapour from the forge
Of a giant somewhere hid,
Out of hearing of the clang
Of his hammer, skirts of mist
Slowly up the woody gorge
Lift and hang.
Softly as a cloud we go,
Sky above and sky below,
Down the river: and the dip
Of the paddles scarcely breaks,
With the little silvery drip
Of the water as it shakes
From the blades, the crystal deep
Of the silence of the morn,
Of the forest yet asleep;
And the river reaches borne
In a mirror, purple gray,
Sheer away
To the misty line of light,
Where the forest and the stream,
In the shadow meet and plight,
Like a dream.
From amid a stretch of reeds,
Where the lazy river sucks
All the water as it bleeds
From a little curling creek,

And the muskrats peer and sneak
In around the sunken wrecks
Of a tree that swept the skies
Long ago,
On a sudden seven ducks
With a splashy rustle rise,
Stretching out their seven necks,
One before, and two behind,
And the others all arow,
And as steady as the wind
With a swivelling whistle go,
Through the purple shadow led,
Till we only hear their whir
In behind a rocky spur,
Just ahead.

ARCHIBALD LAMPMAN

Bab-Lock-Hythe

In the time of wild roses
As up Thames we travelled
Where 'mid water-weeds ravelled
The lily uncloses,

To his old shores the river
A new song was singing,
And young shoots were springing
On old roots for ever.

Dog-daisies were dancing,
And flags flamed in cluster,
On the dark stream a lustre
Now blurred and now glancing.

A tall reed down-weighing
The sedge-warbler fluttered;
One sweet note he uttered,
Then left it soft-swaying.

By the bank's sandy hollow
My dipt oars went beating,
And past our bows fleeting
Blue-backed shone the swallow.

High woods, heron-haunted,
Rose, changed, as we rounded
Old hills greenly mounded,
To meadows enchanted.

A dream ever moulded
Afresh for our wonder,
Still opening asunder
For the stream many-folded;

Till sunset was rimming
The West with pale flushes;
Behind the black rushes
The last light was dimming;

And the lonely stream, hiding
Shy birds, grew more lonely,
And with us was only
The noise of our gliding.

In cloud of gray weather
The evening o'erdarkened.
In the stillness we hearkened;
Our hearts sang together.

LAURENCE BINYON

From The Canoe Speaks

On the great streams the ships may go
About men's business to and fro.
But I, the egg-shell pinnace, sleep
On crystal waters ankle-deep:
I, whose diminutive design,
Of sweeter cedar, pithier pine,
Is fashioned on so frail a mould,
A hand may launch, a hand withhold:
I, rather, with the leaping trout
Wind, among lilies, in and out;
I, the unnamed, inviolate,
Green, rustic rivers navigate;
My dipping paddle scarcely shakes
The berry in the bramble-brakes;
Still forth on my green way I wend
Beside the cottage garden-end;
And by the nested angler fare,
And take the lovers unaware.

ROBERT LOUIS STEVENSON

Canoe

This points through place
gains by a whispered word
and winning no great way
creeps up the tasseled weather of the reeds.

Great boats cut cliffs
and dunk the shoreline land
but this infringes on the willow's shade,
passes the flower's lighthouse, sips the bank.

This that is needle thin
and varnished violin
steered by forgetfulness
through cobweb frontier of the afternoon

gains what the others lose,
Time's primp and pause,
interstices of space
and centimeters sunning on low shores,

while soft sad water beds
curl greenly under it
as in a summer's house
the tufted cavern of an empty grate.

PATRICK ANDERSON

Young Argonauts

In a small bitterness of wind
The reeds divided, as we felt
Our keel slide over stones, and smelt

The lough all round us. Soon the trace
Of shore was further than the sight
Of wildbirds crying in their flight;

But now the waves are paler finned,
The water blacker, we are blown
To somewhere strange and yet foreknown:

This is the Euxine, this the place—
Row on, row on, to catch the gold
In dripping fleece, as they of old.

SHEILA WINGFIELD

Offshore

The bay was anchor, sky,
and island: a land's end
sail, and the world tidal,
that day of blue and boat.

The island swam in the wind
all noon, a seal until
the sun furled down. Orion
loomed, that night, from unfathomed

tides; the flooding sky
was Baltic with thick stars.
On watch for whatever catch,
We coursed that open sea

as if by stars sailed off
the chart; we crewed with Arc-
turus, Vega, Polaris,
tacking into the dark.

PHILIP BOOTH

The Excursion

I

How delightful, at sunset, to loosen the boat!
A light wind is slow to raise waves.
Deep in the bamboo grove, the guests linger;
The lotus-flowers are pure and bright in the cool evening air.
The young nobles stir the ice-water;
The Beautiful Ones wash the lotus-roots, whose fibres are like
    silk threads.
A layer of clouds above our heads is black.
It will certainly rain, which impels me to write this poem.

II

The rain comes, soaking the mats upon which we are sitting.
A hurrying wind strikes the bow of the boat.
The rose-red rouge of the ladies from Yueh is wet;
The Yen beauties are anxious about their kingfisher-eyebrows.
We throw out a rope and draw in to the sloping bank.
    We tie the boat to the willow trees.
We roll up the curtains and watch the floating wave-flowers.
Our return is different from our setting out. The wind whistles
    and blows in great gusts.
By the time we reach the shore, it seems as though the Fifth
    Month were Autumn.

TU FU
Translated by Amy Lowell
and Florence Ayscough

Vacationer

The sailor in his sailboat, homeward bound,
Home from the sea, or anyway the Sound,
Becalmed and parched and grilled and like to fry,
Whistles for wind a good two miles off Rye,
And all those sails that gaily dot the ocean
Rouse in him absolutely no emotion
Except that old vacation boredom, and
A deep desire to be returned to land.

WALKER GIBSON

Sailboat, Your Secret

Sailboat, your secret. With what dove-and-serpent
Craft you trick the old antagonist.
Trick and transpose, snaring him into sponsor.

The blusterer—his blows you twist to blessing.
Your tactics and your tact, O subtle one,
Your war, your peace—you who defer and win.

Not in obeisance, not in defiance you bow,
You bow to him, but in deep irony.
The gull's wing kisses the whitecap not more archly

Than yours. Timeless and motionless I watch
Your craftsmanship, your wiles, O skimmer-schemer,
Your losses to profit, your wayward onwardness.

ROBERT FRANCIS

Come on In

Come on in,
The water's fine.
I'll give you
Till I count nine.
If you're not
In by then,
Guess I'll have to
Count to ten.

OLD RHYME

Yes, by Golly

Yellow-belly, yellow-belly, come and take a swim;
Yes, by golly, when the tide comes in.

OLD RHYME

High Diver

How deep is his duplicity who in a flash
Passes from resting bird to flying bird to fish,

Who momentarily is sculpture, then all motion,
Speed and splash, then climbs again to contemplation.

He is the archer who himself is bow and arrow.
He is the upper-under-world-commuting hero.

His downward going has the air of sacrifice
To some dark seaweed-bearded seagod face to face

Or goddess. Rippling and responsive lies the water
For him to contemplate, then powerfully to enter.

ROBERT FRANCIS

Cold Logic

This man likes to dive
In the cold seasons;
He dives, I suppose,
For divers reasons.

BARNEY HUTCHINSON

142

From Swimmers

Then, the quick plunge into the cool, green dark,
The windy waters rushing past me, through me;
Filled with a sense of some heroic lark,
Exulting in a vigor clean and roomy.
Swiftly I rose to meet the cat-like sea
That sprang upon me with a hundred claws,
And grappled, pulled me down and played with me.
Then, held suspended in the tightening pause
When one wave grows into a toppling acre,
I dived headlong into the foremost breaker,
Pitting against a cold and turbulent strife
The feverish intensity of life.
Out of the foam I lurched and rode the wave,
Swimming, hand over hand, against the wind;
I felt the sea's vain pounding, and I grinned
Knowing I was its master, not its slave.

LOUIS UNTERMEYER

East Anglian Bathe

Oh when the early morning at the seaside
  Took us with hurrying steps from Horsey Mere
To see the whistling bent-grass on the leeside
  And then the tumbled breaker-line appear,
On high, the clouds with mighty adumbration
  Sailed over us to seaward fast and clear
And jellyfish in quivering isolation
  Lay silted in the dry sand of the breeze
And we, along the table-land of beach blown
  Went gooseflesh from our shoulders to our knees
And ran to catch the football, each to each thrown,
  In the soft and swirling music of the seas.

There splashed about our ankles as we waded
  Those interesting wavelets morning-cold,
And sudden dark a patch of sea was shaded,
  And sudden light, another patch would hold
The warmth of whirling atoms in a sun-shot
  And underwater sandstorm green and gold.
So in we dived and louder than a gunshot
  Sea-water broke in fountains down the ear.
How cold the swim, how chattering cold the drying,
  How welcoming the inland reeds appear,
The wood-smoke and the breakfast and the frying,
  And your warm freshwater ripples, Horsey Mere.

JOHN BETJEMAN

144

Ice-Skaters

Snow-hills all about,
And snowy woods; and snow
Falling: a full moon's out;

The river's frozen; across
Its avenue of ice
Vivid skaters swirl

In the cold, in the moon's light.
Look, look: the young, the old,
Set moving by delight.

—The whole town's on the ice!
Whirling in a gay
Preposterous ballet.

Look, the strides, the glides,
Cossack-leaps, dervish-twirls,
Clown-tumblings, clown-falls!

Racers, rapt in speed
As in an ecstasy,
Swerving in a flash of sleet;

Lovers, hand in hand,
Enchanted by their own
Music without sound,

And the older pairs,
A little clumsy now,
But merry as waltzing bears,

And children, intently
Scuffing foot by foot,
Stiffly rocking in and out,

All intricately winding in a Christmas-colored maze
With Lord, what a racket! till the hills
Go wild with echoes, bellow like mad bulls

And in the dark ravines
Beneath the crystal floor
Fish quiver, and wave their fins.

The town clock chimes the hour
Unheeded: let it chime,
Time has lost its power.

What monkey-shines, what fun!
Flesh is no burden now,
It never lay so lightly on the bone.

The body too can be
Spirit, when set free
By pure delight of motion

Without destination;
Shows its own fantasy,
Wit, and imagination.

Is this the being Lear could call
A poor, bare,
Forked animal?

Strike that out; say this,
That in a harsh season,
Above a dark abyss,

The mortal creature
Rejoiced in its own nature;
Revelled, itself the reason.

—Why, life's a carnival! Snow
Falls like confetti now;
The moon, in comic mood,

Turns to a grotesque
Snowball; hides in cloud;
Comes back in a clown's mask.

The skaters swirl and swirl;
All their motions cry
It is joy, sheer joy,

That makes the atoms dance
And wings the flying stars
And speeds the sun upon his golden course.

ELDER OLSON

Skating

. . . So through the darkness and the cold we flew,
And not a voice was idle; with the din
Smitten, the precipices rang aloud;
The leafless trees and every icy crag
Tinkled like iron; while far distant hills
Into the tumult sent an alien sound
Of melancholy not unnoticed, while the stars
Eastward were sparkling clear, and in the west
The orange sky of evening died away.
Not seldom from the uproar I retired
Into a silent bay, or sportively
Glanced sideway, leaving the tumultuous throng,
To cut across the reflex of a star
That fled, and flying still before me, gleamed
Upon the glassy plain; and oftentimes,
When we had given our bodies to the wind,
And all the shadowy banks on either side
Came sweeping through the darkness, spinning still
The rapid line of motion, then at once
Have I, reclining back upon my heels,
Stopped short; yet still the solitary cliffs
Wheeled by me—even as if the earth had rolled
With visible motion her diurnal round!
Behind me did they stretch in solemn train,
Feebler and feebler, and I stood and watched
Till all was tranquil as a dreamless sleep . . .

WILLIAM WORDSWORTH
from The Prelude

The Skaters

Black swallows swooping or gliding
In a flurry of entangled loops and curves;
The skaters skim over the frozen river.
And the grinding click of their skates as they impinge
      upon the surface,
Is like the brushing together of thin wing-tips of silver.

JOHN GOULD FLETCHER

To Kate, Skating Better Than Her Date

Wait, Kate! You skate at such a rate
You leave behind your skating mate.
Your splendid speed won't you abate?
He's lagging far behind you, Kate.
He brought you on this skating date
His shy affection thus to state,
But you on skating concentrate
And leave him with a woeful weight
Pressed on his heart. Oh, what a state
A man gets into, how irate
He's bound to be with life and fate
If, when he tries to promulgate
His love, the loved one turns to skate
Far, far ahead to demonstrate
Superior speed and skill. Oh, hate
Is sure to come of love, dear Kate,
If you so treat your skating mate.
Turn again, Kate, or simply wait
Until he comes, then him berate
(Coyly) for catching up so late.
For, Kate, he *knows* your skating's great,
He's *seen* your splendid figure eight,
He is not here to contemplate
Your supersonic skating rate—
That is not why he made the date.
He's anxious to expatiate
On how he wants you for his mate.
And don't you want to hear him, Kate?

DAVID DAICHES

River Skater

Bound to a boy's swift feet, hard blades of steel
Ring out a brutal rhythm from black ice.
A gawky skater with a godlike heel,
He cuts a clear and convolute device,
A foliated script, nor looks around
To see what letters twine where he has come,
But, all delighted with the savage sound,
His body beats from such a solid drum,
He springs into a faster pace, and then,
Far down the pastures, paper-white and pure,
You see his figure, slanted like a pen,
Writing his own and winter's signature.

WINIFRED WELLES

Skating

Over the ice she flies
Perfect and poised and fair.
Star in my true-love's eyes
Teach me to do and dare.
Now will I fly as she flies—
Woe for the stars that misled.
Stars I beheld in her eyes,
Now do I see in my head!

RUDYARD KIPLING

Fast

Two people
like sailboats on an icy lake
skating imitating angels bumped
    in the radiance of beauty.
    Picking themselves up
    and seeing clouds
    they remember spring
    and return like
    birds to the flight
    on the reflection of heaven.

JOHN TAGLIABUE

Skier

He swings down like the flourish of a pen
Signing a signature in white on white.

The silence of his skis reciprocates
The silence of the world around him.

Wind is his one competitor
In the cool winding and unwinding down.

On incandescent feet he falls
Unfalling, trailing white foam, white fire.

ROBERT FRANCIS

152

Winter Trees

I think that I shall never ski
Again against so stout a tree.

A tree whose rugged bark is pressed
In bas-relief upon my chest.

A tree that with bacchantic air
Wears ski poles in its tangled hair.
. . . . .
I've learned my lesson: Fools like me
Should never try to shave a tree.

CONRAD DIEKMANN

Instruction in the Art

Great things are done when men and mountains meet;
This is not done by jostling in the street.

WILLIAM BLAKE

Instruction in the Art

"TAKE A BOY FISHING"

Boy, the giant beauty
that you cast for lies
upstream in this same current
that you wade. Men wise
with love have wintered
on the iron bridge, dreamed
opening day, and tied
their hatful of bright
artificial flies.

This is an old one, boy,
not in memory struck
at a false cast. No, nor
felt the quick-set hook.
The snags are ragged
with lost lures, hair and
gold; even icons shaped
like a woman, this beauty
never took.

Boy, cast lightly. Long
and lightly where the shallow
split tongue of current
undercuts the meadow;
in that spun pool
where blue flowers overhang
the bank, by first light

a few quiet men at last
have seen the shadow.

We only guess, boy,
by the stream-run shape
of steelheads, or a rainbow
beached in winter sleep.
Such forms lose color
in the creel; men file
barbs not toward food
or trophies, but for luck
they cannot keep.

Boy, the giant beauty
that you cast for lies
upstream. I pray you patience
for that tug and rise,
the risen image
that outleaps the rapids
in one illimitable
arc: to praise,
but not to prize.

PHILIP BOOTH

Neither Hook nor Line

You see the ways the fisherman doth take
To catch the fish; what engines doth he make!
Behold! how he engageth all his wits;
Also his snares, lines, angles, hooks and nets;
Yet fish there be, that neither hook nor line,
Nor snare, nor net, nor engine, can make thine:
They must be groped for, and be tickled too,
Or they will not be catch'd, whate'er you do.

JOHN BUNYAN
(1678)

Old Tennis Player

Refuses
To refuse the racket, to mutter No to the net.
He leans to life, conspires to give and get
Other serving yet.

GWENDOLYN BROOKS

Villanelle

You cannot rest behind the plate,
The ball has caught the batter's eye.
Unmask and be the sport of fate.

To crouch were best, if one could wait,
But runners break and cast the die.
You cannot rest behind the plate.

No mortal can anticipate
The all-resolving infield fly.
Unmask and be the sport of fate.

The reasoned act is often late.
One blow can shatter all your sky.
You cannot rest behind the plate.

Foul or passed ball immolate
The hero who has failed to try.
Unmask and be the sport of fate.

Weep, O Lowly! Exult, ye Great!
The rules do not permit a tie.
You cannot rest behind the plate.
Unmask and be the sport of fate.

M. D. FELD

Athletic Employment

To live a life, free from gout, pain, and phthisic,
Athletic employment is found the best physic;
The nerves are by exercise hardened and strengthened,
And vigour attends it by which life is lengthened.

OLD BALLAD

Who Misses or Who Wins

Who misses or who wins the prize
Go lose or conquer as you can;
But if you fall, or if you rise,
Be each, pray God, a gentleman.

WILLIAM MAKEPEACE THACKERAY

Reflections Outside of a Gymnasium

The belles of the eighties were soft,
  They were ribboned and ruffled and gored,
With bustles built proudly aloft
  And bosoms worn dashingly for'rd.
So, doting on bosoms and bustles,
  By fashion and circumstance pent,
They languished, neglecting their muscles,
  Growing flabby and plump and content,
Their most strenuous sport
  A game of croquet
On a neat little court
  In the cool of the day,
Or dipping with ladylike motions,
Fully clothed, into decorous oceans.

The eighties surveyed with alarm
  A figure long-legged and thinnish;
And they had not discovered the charm
  Of a solid-mahogany finish.
Of suns that could darken or speckle
  Their delicate skins they were wary.
They found it distasteful to freckle
  Or brown like a nut or a berry.
So they sat in the shade
  Or they put on a hat
And frequently stayed
  Fairly healthy at that
(And never lay nightlong awake
For sunburn and loveliness' sake).

When ladies rode forth, it was news,
   Though sidewise ensconced on the saddle.
And when they embarked in canoes
   A gentleman wielded the paddle.
They never felt urged to compete
   With persons excessively agile.
Their slippers were small on their feet
   And they thought it no shame to be fragile.
Could they swim? They could not.
Did they dive? They forbore it.
And nobody thought
   The less of them for it.

No, none pointed out how their course was absurd,
Though their tennis was feeble, their golf but a word.
When breezes were chilly, they wrapped up in flannels,
They couldn't turn cartwheels, they didn't swim channels,
They seldom climbed mountains, and, what was more shocking,
Historians doubt that they even went walking.
If unenergetic,
   A demoiselle dared to
Be no more athletic
   Than ever she cared to.
Oh, strenuous comrades and maties,
How pleasant was life in the eighties!

PHYLLIS MC GINLEY

162

The Breed of Athletes

Of the myriad afflictions that beset Hellas
none is worse than the breed of athletes.
Never, first of all, do they understand the good life,
nor could they. How can a man ensiaved to his jaws,
subject to his belly, increase his patrimony?
Nor to abide poverty, to row in fortune's stream
are they able; they have not learned the fair art
of confronting the insoluble. Shining in youth
they stride about like statues in the square.
But comes astringent age, they shrink in rags.
Blameworthy is the custom of the Hellenes
who for such men make great concourses
to honor idle sports—for feasting's sake.
What nimble wrestler, fleet runner, sinewy
discus thrower, agile boxer, has benefited his city
by his firsts? Fight our enemy discus in hand?
In mellay of shields box the foe from the fatherland?
Confronted with steel, such silliness none remembers.
'Tis the wise and the good we should crown with bay,
who best guide the state, the prudent and the just,
whoso by discourse averts evil actions, banishes
strife and contention. Prowess of such sort
is to all the city a boon, to all Hellenes.

EURIPIDES
Translated by Moses Hadas

Civilities

The delicate corner shot,
Slicing the strings precise across the ball
At the right time, so that it lightly hits
    On one side wall,
    Kisses the front, then falls
Quick-dying down, most irretrievable,

    Is difficult to do
Unless a calm, an inner certainty
Comes to you softly in the midst of war,
    Setting you free
    From the slam-bang desire
To smash it hard no matter where. To be

    So deftly sure, so wise,
Wins points in squash. In another, harder game,
Word-play, a similar civility
    May equally tame
    Peaceless desires, and make
Your opponent yours by a nicety of name.

THOMAS WHITBREAD

First Lesson

Lie back, daughter, let your head
be tipped back in the cup of my hand.
Gently, and I will hold you. Spread
your arms wide, lie out on the stream
and look high at the gulls. A dead-
man's-float is face down. You will dive
and swim soon enough where this tidewater
ebbs to the sea. Daughter, believe
me, when you tire on the long thrash
to your island, lie up, and survive.
As you float now, where I held you
and let go, remember when fear
cramps your heart what I told you:
lie gently and wide to the light-year
stars, lie back, and the sea will hold you.

PHILIP BOOTH

165

The Road All Runners Come

"Is football playing
  Along the river shore,
With lads to chase the leather,
  Now I stand up no more?"

A. E. HOUSMAN

To an Athlete Dying Young

The time you won your town the race
We chaired you through the market-place;
Man and boy stood cheering by,
And home we brought you shoulder-high.

Today, the road all runners come,
Shoulder-high we bring you home,
And set you at your threshold down,
Townsman of a stiller town.

Smart lad, to slip betimes away
From fields where glory does not stay
And early though the laurel grows
It withers quicker than the rose.

Eyes the shady night has shut
Cannot see the record cut,
And silence sounds no worse than cheers
After earth has stopped the ears;

Now you will not swell the rout
Of lads that wore their honour out,
Runners whom renown outran
And the name died before the man.

So set, before its echoes fade,
The fleet foot on the sill of shade,
And hold to the low lintel up
The still defended challenge-cup.

And round that early-laurelled head
Will flock to gaze the strengthless dead
And find unwithered on its curls
The garland briefer than a girl's.

A. E. HOUSMAN

That Dark Other Mountain

My father could go down a mountain faster than I
Though I was first one up.
Legs braced or with quick steps he slid the gravel slopes
Where I picked cautious footholds.

Black, Iron, Eagle, Doublehead, Chocorua,
Wildcat and Carter Dome—
He beat me down them all. And that last other mountain
And that dark other mountain.

ROBERT FRANCIS

For E. McC.

THAT WAS MY COUNTER-BLADE UNDER
LEONARDO TERRONE, MASTER OF FENCE

Gone while your tastes were keen to you,
Gone where the grey winds call to you,
By that high fencer, even Death,
Struck of the blade that no man parrieth;
Such is your fence, one saith,
    One that hath known you.
Drew you your sword most gallantly
Made you your pass most valiantly
    'Gainst that grey fencer, even Death.

Gone as a gust of breath
Faith! no man tarrieth,
'Se il cor ti manca,' but it failed thee not!
'Non ti fidar,' it is the sword that speaks
'In me.' *
Thou trusted'st in thyself and met the blade
'Thout mask or gauntlet, and art laid
As memorable broken blades that be
Kept as bold trophies of old pageantry.

* 'Se il cor ti manca, non ti fidar
in me.' 'If thy heart fail thee,
trust not in me.' (Sword-rune)

As old Toledos past their days of war
Are kept mnemonic of the strokes they bore,
So art thou with us, being good to keep
In our heart's sword-rack, though thy sword-arm sleep.

ENVOI

Struck of the blade that no man parrieth,
Pierced of the point that toucheth lastly all,
'Gainst that grey fencer, even Death,
Behold the shield! He shall not take thee all.

EZRA POUND

In the beginning was the

Kickoff.
The ball flew
spiralling true
into the end zone
where it was snagged,
neatly hugged
by a swivel-hipped back
who ran up the field
and was smeared.

The game has begun.
The game has been won.
The game goes on.
Long live the game.
Gather and lock
tackle and block
move, move,
around the arena
and always the beautiful
trajectories.

LEE MURCHISON

172

The Ageing Athlete

You're through—now walking up and down,
you think of speed and dig your heels,
testing this soil and that for a start,
but it's no go . . . Practicing for leaps,
you start forward, but exhaust the push
and end up with a damaging rush,
arms hanging, hands twitching at your sides,
chin bobbing on your chest: no pride
that once sustained you as you leapt
the next hurdle, hair up then down,
the wind in your ears, the crowd beside
itself, shouting, Come on! Come on!
and you smashed the tape with your chest
and sank into the arms of many lovers.

NEIL WEISS

The Convict of Clonmel

How hard is my fortune,
  And vain my repining;
The strong rope of fate
  For this young neck is twining!
My strength is departed,
  My cheeks sunk and sallow,
While I languish in chains
  In the jail of Clonmala.

No boy of the village
  Was ever yet milder;
I'd play with a child
  And my sport would be wilder;
I'd dance without tiring
  From morning till even,
And the goal-ball I'd strike
  To the lightning of Heaven.

At my bed-foot decaying,
  My hurl-bat is lying;
Through the boys of the village
  My goal-ball is flying;
My horse 'mong the neighbors
  Neglected may fallow,
While I pine in my chains
  In the jail of Clonmala.

Next Sunday the patron°
   At home will be keeping,
And the young active hurlers
   The field will be sweeping;
With the dance of fair maidens
   The evening they'll hallow,
While this heart, once so gay,
   Shall be cold in Clonmala.

J. J. CALLANAN
Translated from the Irish

° Patron—Irish *patruin*—a festive gathering
of the people on tented ground.

At Grass

The eye can hardly pick them out
From the cold shade they shelter in,
Till wind distresses tail and mane;
Then one crops grass, and moves about
—The other seeming to look on—
And stands anonymous again.

Yet fifteen years ago, perhaps
Two dozen distances sufficed
To fable them: faint afternoons
Of Cups and Stakes and Handicaps,
Whereby their names were artificed
To inlay faded, classic Junes—

Silks at the start: against the sky
Numbers and parasols: outside,
Squadrons of empty cars, and heat,
And littered grass: then the long cry
Hanging unhushed till it subside
To stop-press columns on the street.

Do memories plague their ears like flies?
They shake their heads. Dusk brims the shadows.
Summer by summer all stole away,
The starting gates, the crowds and cries—
All but the unmolesting meadows.
Almanacked, their names live; they

Have slipped their names, and stand at ease,
Or gallop for what must be joy,
And not a fieldglass sees them home,
Or curious stop-watch prophesies:
Only the groom, and the groom's boy,
With bridles in the evening come.

PHILIP LARKIN

Athletes

The groggy fighter on his knees
Sways up at nine, postpones the count;
The jockey, forty-to-one shot, sees
Them all go by, yet whips his mount;
The losing pitcher, arm gone lame,
Still drops that last one in, a strike—
So you and I play a stubborn game,
Disaster prodding us alike.
So you and I, ignoring odds,
Tug caps, clutch ropes, and flail our whips,
Make sacrifices to the gods,
Breed children and build battleships,
Though ours is not an athlete's doom,
Nor death like any shower room.

WALKER GIBSON

The Old Swimmer

I often wander on the beach
Where once, so brown of limb,
The biting air, the roaring surf
Summoned me to swim.

I see my old abundant youth
Where combers lean and spill,
And though I taste the foam no more
Other swimmers will.

Oh, good exultant strength to meet
The arching wall of green,
To break the crystal, swirl, emerge
Dripping, taut, and clean.

To climb the moving hilly blue,
To dive in ecstasy
And feel the salty chill embrace
Arm and rib and knee.

What brave and vanished laughter then
And tingling thighs to run,
What warm and comfortable sands
Dreaming in the sun.

The crumbling water spreads in snow,
The surf is hissing still,
And though I kiss the salt no more
Other swimmers will.

CHRISTOPHER MORLEY

The Skaters

Graceful and sure with youth, the skaters glide
Upon the frozen pond. Unending rings
Expand upon the ice, contract, divide,
Till motion seems the shape that movement brings,

And shape is constant in the moving blade.
Ignorant of the beauty they invent,
Confirmed in their hard strength, the youths evade
Their frail suspension on an element,

This frozen pond that glisters in the cold.
Through all the warming air they turn and spin,
And do not feel that they grow old
Above the fragile ice they scrape and thin.

JOHN WILLIAMS

Hunting Song

Waken, lords and ladies gay,
On the mountain dawns the day,
All the jolly chase is here,
With hawk and horse and hunting-spear!
Hounds are in their couples yelling,
Hawks are whistling, horns are knelling,
Merrily, merrily, mingle they,
"Waken, lords and ladies gay."

Waken, lords and ladies gay,
The mist has left the mountain gray,
Springlets in the dawn are steaming,
Diamonds on the brake are gleaming:
And foresters have busy been
To track the buck in thicket green;
Now we come to chant our lay,
"Waken, lords and ladies gay."

Waken, lords and ladies gay,
To the greenwood haste away;
We can show you where he lies,
Fleet of foot and tall of size;
We can show the marks he made,
When 'gainst the oak his antlers frayed;
You shall see him brought to bay,
"Waken, lords and ladies gay."

Louder, louder chant the lay,
Waken, lords and ladies gay!

Tell them youth and mirth and glee
Run a course as well as we;
Time, stern huntsman, who can balk,
Stanch as hound and fleet as hawk?
Think of this and rise with day,
Gentle lords and ladies gay.

SIR WALTER SCOTT

I Bless This Man

I bless this man for Agesilas, his father,
for the splendor and linked serenity of his limbs.
Yet if one, keeping wealth, surpass in beauty likewise
and show his strength by excellence in the games,
let him remember the limbs he appoints are mortal
and that he must put upon him earth, the end of all things.

In the speech of good citizens he should win praise
and be a theme of elaboration in the deep, sweet singing.

PINDAR
from Nemea 11
Translated by Richmond Lattimore

Into Lucid Air

I inhale great draughts of space,
The east and the west are mine, and the
   north and the south are mine.

WALT WHITMAN

A Kite Is a Victim

A kite is a victim you are sure of.
You love it because it pulls
gentle enough to call you master,
strong enough to call you fool;
because it lives
like a desperate trained falcon
in the high sweet air,
and you can always haul it down
to tame it in your drawer.

A kite is a fish you have already caught
in a pool where no fish come,
so you play him carefully and long,
and hope he won't give up,
or the wind die down.

A kite is the last poem you've written,
so you give it to the wind,
but you don't let it go
until someone finds you
something else to do.

A kite is a contract of glory
that must be made with the sun,
so you make friends with the field
the river and the wind,
then you pray the whole cold night before,
under the travelling cordless moon,
to make you worthy and lyric and pure.

LEONARD COHEN

Spring Is a Looping-Free Time

Boys like puppets dangling
On the drooping curves of baseballs;
Babies in swings who swoop
To float in chains back to mothers;
Pole-vaulters scooped-up
To poise, prouder than Icarus.

Even the scarring-white trails of jets
Can't splinter the sky's prayer into angles
Or recall winter's prison-square penance.
Not while the sun and a southerly breeze
Are shining and blueing the heavens
Cleaner than Sunday, warmer than leaves.

MARTIN ROBBINS

All in Green Went My Love Riding

All in green went my love riding
on a great horse of gold
into the silver dawn.

four lean hounds crouched low and smiling
the merry deer ran before.

Fleeter be they than dappled dreams
the swift sweet deer
the red rare deer.

Four red roebuck at a white water
the cruel bugle sang before.

Horn at hip went my love riding
riding the echo down
into the silver dawn.

four lean hounds crouched low and smiling
the level meadows ran before.

Softer be they than slippered sleep
the lean lithe deer
the fleet flown deer.

Four fleet does at a gold valley
the famished arrow sang before.

Bow at belt went my love riding
riding the mountain down
into the silver dawn.

four lean hounds crouched low and smiling
the sheer peaks ran before.

Paler be they than daunting death
the sleek slim deer
the tall tense deer.

Four tall stags at a green mountain
The lucky hunter sang before.

All in green went my love riding
on a great horse of gold
into the silver dawn.

four lean hounds crouched low and smiling
my heart fell dead before.

                              E. E. CUMMINGS

The Bait

Come, live with me, and be my love,
And we will some new pleasures prove,
Of golden sands, and crystal brooks,
With silken lines, and silver hooks.

There will the river whisp'ring run,
Warm'd by thy eyes more than the sun;
And there the enamoured fish will stay,
Begging themselves they may betray.

When thou wilt swim in that live bath,
Each fish, which every channel hath,
Most amorously to thee will swim,
Gladder to catch thee, than thou him.

If thou, to be so seen, beest loath
By sun or moon, thou dark'nest both;
And if mine eyes have leave to see,
I need not their light, having thee.

Let others freeze with angling reeds,
And cut their legs with shells and weeds,
Or treacherously poor fish beset
With strangling snares or windowy net;

Let coarse bold hands, from slimy nest,
The bedded fish in banks outwrest;
Or curious traitors, sleave silk flies,
Bewitch poor wand'ring fishes' eyes.

For thee, thou need'st no such deceit,
For thou thyself art thine own bait;
That fish, that is not catch'd thereby,
Is wiser far, alas, than I.

JOHN DONNE

Life Is Motion

In Oklahoma,
Bonnie and Josie,
Dressed in calico,
Danced around a stump.
They cried,
"Ohoyaho,
Ohoo" . . .
Celebrating the marriage
Of flesh and air.

WALLACE STEVENS

The Runner

Suddenly with intense
feet he moves by motion
and no sound to round

the corner heading
North; the pure cold
lost last place, his head

lost too between
the sharp uncertain flowers
of the high air and

the harshest mountain
flutesong for his breath O
helmeted with hair

he rides the silhouette
of stylized ecstasy
until untranced he stops

but his heart runs.

ALEXANDRA GRILIKHES

At Galway Races

There where the course is,
Delight makes all of the one mind,
The riders upon the galloping horses,
The crowd that closes in behind:
We, too, had good attendance once,
Hearers and hearteners of the work;
Aye, horsemen for companions,
Before the merchant and the clerk
Breathed on the world with timid breath.
Sing on: somewhere at some new moon,
We'll learn that sleeping is not death,
Hearing the whole earth change its tune,
Its flesh being wild, and it again
Crying aloud as the racecourse is,
And we find hearteners among men
That ride upon horses.

WILLIAM BUTLER YEATS

The Fisherman

Although I can see him still,
The freckled man who goes
To a grey place on a hill
In grey Connemara clothes
At dawn to cast his flies,
It's long since I began
To call up to the eyes
This wise and simple man.
All day I'd looked in the face
What I had hoped 'twould be
To write for my own race
And the reality;
The living men that I hate,
The dead man that I loved,
The craven man in his seat,
The insolent unreproved,
And no knaves brought to book
Who has won a drunken cheer,
The witty man and his joke
Aimed at the commonest ear,
The clever man who cries
The catch-cries of the clown,
The beating down of the wise
And great Art beaten down.

Maybe a twelvemonth since
Suddenly I began,
In scorn of this audience,
Imagining a man,

And his sun-freckled face,
And grey Connemara cloth,
Climbing up to a place
Where stone is dark under froth,
And the down-turn of his twist
When the flies drop in the stream;
A man who does not exist,
A man who is but a dream;
And cried, 'Before I am old
I shall have written him one
Poem maybe as cold
And passionate as the dawn.'

WILLIAM BUTLER YEATS

Prayer

God who created me
   Nimble and light of limb,
In three elements free,
   To run, to ride, to swim:
Not when the sense is dim,
   But now from the heart of joy,
I would remember Him:
   Take the thanks of a boy.

HENRY CHARLES BEECHING

Black Water and Bright Air

Skaters upon thin ice,
how weightlessly they leap,
like figures seen in sleep;
how rhythmic, how precise
the pattern of their skates
upon the frozen floor—
the shell that separates
black water and bright air,
the shell beneath which waits,
dreadful and disavowed,
an element forsworn.
Oh, but the skaters know
the sullen depths below;
they test what can be borne;
their bodies, like their breath,
floating on winter air,
lightly they skim and soar
from shore to barren shore,
lightness their one device,
their article of faith.

O summer, come once more!
Season of innocence,
under the summer cloud,
join air and water, let
the severed elements,
with no more parting, fuse;
set the bound water loose,
let those who feared its threat

dare to plunge downward, straight
through waters warm and bright
into that cold unknown,
deeper and deeper down,
terrified, into black,
until they touch the stone,
touch the bleak stone at last;
then, only then, turn back,
turn toward the sky, released,
borne upward toward the sun
through layers of lessening weight,
back into summer light,
back into lucid air.

CONSTANCE CARRIER

ACKNOWLEDGMENTS

For permission to use certain poems in this anthology, grateful acknowledgment is made to the following:

SAMUEL W. ALLEN for "To Satch (or American Gothic)" from *Soon, One Morning* edited by Herbert Hill, copyright © 1963, Alfred A. Knopf, Inc.

PHILIP BOOTH for "Offshore" (*The Atlantic Monthly*, January, 1964).

MRS. VIRGINIA LEE WARREN BRACKER and THE NEW YORK TIMES for "Where, O Where?" and "The Umpire" by Milton Bracker, © 1962 by The New York Times Company.

CURTIS BROWN, LTD. for 46 lines of commentary by W. H. Auden from the film *Runner,* copyright © 1962 by the National Film Board of Canada, reprinted by permission of the author; for "The Hunter" and "Line-Up for Yesterday" from *Versus,* by Ogden Nash, copyright © 1947, 1949, by Ogden Nash, reprinted by permission of the author.

JOHN BRUCE and THE FIDDLEHEAD for "The Pike."

WITTER BYNNER for "A Green Stream" by Wang Wei, translated by Witter Bynner and Kiang Kang-hu (*Poetry*, February, 1922).

THE CRESSET PRESS LIMITED for "Young Argonauts" from *A Kite's Dinner: Poems 1938–1954* by Sheila Wingfield.

BABETTE DEUTSCH for "Morning Workout," reprinted by permission of the author, from *New Poems by American Poets, No. 2*, edited by Rolfe Humphries, © 1957 Ballantine Books, Inc.

THE DIAL PRESS for "Settling Some Old Football Scores" from *A Bowl of Bishop* by Morris Bishop, copyright © 1954 by Morris Bishop, reprinted by permission of The Dial Press, Inc.

ALAN DUGAN for "On Hurricane Jackson" from *Poems* by Alan Dugan, Yale University Press, © 1961 by Alan Dugan.

E. P. DUTTON & CO., INC., for "Eight Oars and a Coxswain," from the book *Ballads of Old New York* by Arthur Guiterman, copyright, 1939, by E. P. Dutton & Co., Inc., reprinted by permission of the publisher.

THE ESTATE OF FRANKLIN P. ADAMS for "Baseball Note" from *Nods and Becks* by Franklin P. Adams, copyright 1944, and for "Baseball's Sad Lexicon," copyright 1936.

FARRAR, STRAUS & COMPANY, INC., for "The Closing of the Rodeo," reprinted from *Celebration at Dark* by William Jay Smith, by permission of Farrar, Straus & Company, Inc., all rights reserved.

M. D. FELD for "Villanelle." Original poem reprinted by permission of the author.

THE SYNDICS OF THE FITZWILLIAM MUSEUM, CAMBRIDGE, *for* "The Old Squire" by Wilfrid Scawen Blunt.

198

200

P. G. WODEHOUSE and WILLIAM COLE for "Afforestation" by E. A. Wodehouse.
ANN WOLFE for "The Boxer's Face," "The Sluggard," and "The World's Worst
Boxer" by Lucilius, translated by Humbert Wolfe. Reprinted from *Others
Abide* by Humbert Wolfe (Ernest Benn, Ltd.).

"The Ball and the Club" by Forbes Lindsay is from *Lyrics of the Links*
by Henry Litchfield West, © 1921 The Macmillan Company.
The lines by Pindar on p. 51 are from *The Odes of Pindar* translated by
Richmond Lattimore © 1947 by The University of Chicago.
"Football Song" by Sir Walter Scott is an excerpt from his "Lines on the
Lifting of the Banner of the House of Buccleuch, at a Great Football Match
on Carterhaugh."

INDEX OF AUTHORS

INDEX OF FIRST LINES

INDEX OF TITLES

INDEX BY SPORT

210

About the Compiler

LILLIAN MORRISON was born in Jersey City, New Jersey. As a librarian she has worked with young people for many years and is assistant coordinator of Young Adult Services at the New York Public Library. Miss Morrison is the general editor of the Crowell Poets series and has compiled several excellent anthologies of popular folk rhymes.

She was graduated Phi Beta Kappa from Douglass College with a B.S. in mathematics, and received her library degree from Columbia University. Poetry, language, jazz, the dance, and sports are particular interests of hers. She plays tennis and golf, and enjoys most other sports as a spectator.

About the Artists

CLARE ROMANO ROSS and JOHN ROSS were trained at the Cooper Union School of Art and studied at the Ecole des Beaux Arts, Fontainebleau, France, and at the Istituto Statale, Florence, Italy. The Rosses were awarded Tiffany Fellowships for printmaking and lived in Italy for a year under a Fulbright grant for woodcuts. They are represented in museums throughout the United States and their work is in the permanent collection of the Metropolitan Museum of Art.

Mr. and Mrs. Ross live and work in New Jersey, a short distance from New York City where they teach.